# Parallel Dreams Alpine Skiing

## Taking your skiing performance to new levels

DEREK TATE

**Parallel Dreams Publishing**

**Principle author:** Derek Tate

**Contributing writers:** Robbie Fenlon, Professor David Murrie, Shona Tate & Liam Williams

**Main demonstrators:** Siobhain Duggan, Robbie Fenlon, Colm Higgins, David Murrie, Deirdre O'Neill, Derek Tate, Shona Tate & Liam Williams

**Photography** (unless otherwise stated): Robbie Fenlon, Deirdre O'Neill, Alasdair Scobbie, Derek Tate & Shona Tate

Front cover design by Printwize; www.printwize.co.uk
Typesetting: William Murray; dubmail@iol.ie
Printed by: ColourBooks Ltd. www.colourbooks.ie

Published and distributed in the UK & Ireland by:
**Parallel Dreams Publishing**
derek@paralleldreams.co.uk
www.paralleldreams.co.uk

**ISBN: 978-0-9556251-0-7**

*Front cover photo: Derek Tate skiing la Vallée Blanche, Chamonix
Photo by Shona Tate*

This book is dedicated to
Andrew Smart
A true friend, skier and lover of life
Your spirit lives on

# Table of Contents  Page No.

# Table of Contents                                    Page No.

NB: All Segments (or parts of) by Derek Tate unless otherwise stated.

## Forward – by Andrew Lockerbie

Skiing meets the needs of many people in many different ways; exhilaration, challenging, to be technically perfect, and at any standard you can get immense pleasure and yet never feel satisfied as you always wish for more. The instructor takes on the role to achieve all of these for the client.

The Instructor ensures that the client always realises when the success that they once wished for has been achieved, even if the client and instructor is one in the same, you!

What all instructors have is the drive to get the best out of their clients and pass on their own enthusiasm for the sport. Derek Tate is second to none in the drive for self improvement and the improvement of others. Derek has proved this over the years attaining the highest international qualifications and holding positions such as BASI Trainer, Snowsports Scotland Tutor and Director of Training for the Irish Association of Snowsports Instructors. Having spent many seasons over the years teaching many hundreds of clients, Derek has brought together some of the best, including his wife Shona, to impart his and their profound knowledge to thousands who would like to enjoy the sport as much as themselves.

I wish Derek and Shona every success with this book, (which I am sure will be the first of many), and all their other interests that they have in the world of snowsports.

By reading this book you will be able to improve yourself and others. By keeping it as a reference manual you will gain more and more from each time you read it.

# Introduction – Why another skiing book?

There have been many books written about skiing and many technical manuals produced by snowsports instructor training bodies so why produce yet another one?

Firstly there are not that many skiing books written by Irish skiers and as I hail from Dublin and have made skiing and ski teaching my career for over twenty years I feel I have gained a valuable insight into the world of skiing and I have seen the sport evolve as longer narrow skis were replaced by shorter shaped carving skis. Secondly I have had the privilege of being involved with the Irish Association of Snowsports Instructors (IASI) during much of this time, as it has grown from the artificial slopes of Dublin to a full training & grading system recognised by International Snowsport bodies and employers. And it is in my current role as IASI Director of Training that I feel we need a technical book which helps to underpin our system.

The content of this book is based on my experiences and the influence of many skiers, ski teachers and trainers of instructors. While there are many people that I could mention there are a few that stand out from the rest; Paddy Roche from the Ski Club of Ireland in Dublin who provided so much support and encouragement when I was starting out, Dougie Bryce who fulfilled that role as I started my teaching career in Scotland, Alan McGregor who was one of the most inspirational and technically gifted skiers I have ever watched and John Arnold the modern day guru who truly fulfilled the "coaching" role and helped me become both skier and ski teacher.

And while there have been many books written about skiing there are definitely some that have made a big impact on the world of skiing and really helped me to understand how skiing works; Skilful Skiing by John Shedden and How the Racers Ski by Warren Witherall.

And finally while it may seem a little tacky the ski movie of all time has to be "The Blizzard of Ahhs" centred round Chamonix where I now live and run my own ski school.

*Team Salomon during the photo shoot for the book at les Grands Montets, Argentière.*
*Back row (from left to right), Shona Tate, Alastair Henry, Siobhain Duggan & Colm Higgins. Front row (from left to right), Liam Williams, Deirdre O'Neill, Derek Tate & Dave Murrie.*

*Photo by Alasdair Scobbie*

# About the writers

## Principle Author

### Derek Tate

Derek is the current Director of Training for IASI. Originally from Dublin, Derek has been teaching skiing full time for over 20 years. He has been instrumental in developing the training and grading system for IASI. He also works as a trainer for the British Association of Snowsport Instructors (BASI). He now lives in Chamonix where he runs his ski school together with his wife Shona.

Derek's career started on the artificial slope at Kilternan, Dublin where the Ski Club of Ireland are based. Having done his first BASI course in January 1986 in Flaine, France, he then taught his first three seasons in the Cairngorm Mountains of Scotland working for Carrbridge Ski School. Since then Derek has worked in many parts of the world from New Hampshire, USA to Chatel in the Portes du Soleil, and Courchevel in three valleys of France to name but a few.

Derek is also a graduate of the Diploma in Professional Studies Sports Coaching, from Moray House/Heriot Watt University in Edinburgh, Scotland. And he represented Ireland as a technical delegate at the 1999 Interski Congress in Norway.

Writing this book has been a natural development of Derek's career following the writing of educational resources for BASI, Snowsport Scotland and IASI.

## Contributing Writers

### Shona Tate

Shona is co-director of the British Alpine Ski School Chamonix (BASS Chamonix). She is a former Scottish Alpine Ski Team member and current BASI Trainer. She is a member of IASI and a full alpine trainer for the association where she regularly delivers courses on snow and artificial slopes.

Shona's skiing career started at the age of 2 in the Cairngorms and ski racing naturally followed on. Having competed at National and International level, race coaching was the next step, with her initial experience gained at Glenshee, another of the Scottish ski resorts.

More recent experience has included working for New Generation Ski School in Courchevel, tutoring instructor and leadership courses for Snowsport Scotland and delivering BASI Instructor courses.

### Robbie Fenlon

Robbie is a UIAGM Mountain Guide and lives in Chamonix. Originally from Ireland he has helped to promote Chamonix as a winter & summer destination for the Irish. He writes regularly for "Outsider" Irelands' Outdoor Adventure magazine. He is a current trainer for IASI delivering the Off Piste Mountain Safety

modules. He is the founding director of Wilderplaces, which offers mountaineering courses in many places around the world. As a keen skier, Robbie has been instrumental in developing backcountry courses and three years ago teamed up with Derek Tate and his ski school BASS Chamonix to run these courses combining the best of guiding and ski teaching.

### Professor David Murrie

Specialising in biomechanics and coach education, David has been a Head of Sport and Exercise Sciences in Universities in England and Scotland for 10 years. Born in Manchester, David is a graduate of Loughborough University and was a national level athlete. He is an experienced physical education teacher and has coached and given sports science and fitness advice in a wide variety of settings including professional football, World Championship athletics and the British Ski Academy.

Despite not starting skiing until the age of 31, David is an internationally qualified ski teacher. A member of IASI he has pioneered and delivered the IASI Coaching Theory module.

David is currently a professor in biomechanics at Valdosta State University in the United States where he is developing a new Ed.S. (a post Masters level) degree in Sports Coaching.

### Liam Williams

Liam is a former Olympian competing as a coxswain in the coxed pair event in both the Moscow Olympics in 1980 and the Seoul Olympics in 1988 in the sport of rowing. He represented Ireland at 2 world rowing championships in 1979 and 1987. He also has two national intermediate championships and fourteen senior championships.

Having retired from competitive rowing, he took up skiing in 1996. He is now an internationally qualified ski teacher and member of IASI and current trainer for the IASI level 1 ski instructor courses.

Liam competed at various sports and continues to train on a daily basis and is currently competing in triathlons.

*Les Grands Montets, Argentière, in all its grandeur. Skiing is far more than just technique!*

*Dave Murrie skiing at les Grands Montets, Argentière*

*Photo by Alasdair Scobbie*

# Segment 1 – Basic Principles of Skiing

All sports are based around basic principles which underpin efficient and effective performance. Understanding and applying these principles is essential for skiers and teachers alike if they are to get the maximum enjoyment from the sport. This first segment of the book focuses on these principles and looks more closely at the relationship between balancing and movements as well as validating this with sound biomechanics.

## 1.1    Balancing & Movements

Skiing can be both simple and complex. The goal of this part of segment one is to take some complex concepts and make them as easy to understand as possible. In essence there are four key areas that we need to look at;

- The **Forces** that are acting on you as you ski
- The **Movements** that you can make
- The process of **Balancing**
- And how to **Steer** your skis so that you make fluently linked curves

### Forces acting on you as you ski

This is an area that can become very complex and there are a number of texts that cover this in great detail such as "The Skiers Edge" and "Skilful Skiing" (see the references at the back of this book). Professor David Murrie covers this in greater detail in the next part of this book under the heading "Biomechanics". For now we simply need to understand the effects of sliding downhill and turning left and right e.g., the external forces acting on you and how you respond to them.

Gravity, snow resistance and centripetal force are examples of these. Internal forces generated by the skier using his / her muscles come under what we call kinesiology and are dealt with throughout the technical sections of this book.

**Gravity** is the force which creates momentum. Because you are sliding down a mountain and gravity is continually pulling your body (mass) towards the ground, momentum is created. When you turn your skis left or right you must resist gravities pull. As you do this the snow is compressed causing **snow resistance**. It is because of this interaction between the skis and the snow that you feel the force pushing back up from the snow through the bottoms of your skis and up through your body.

The design of skis also plays an important role here because as you tilt and turn your skis, the skis bend into reverse camber and are forced around the curve. The force that causes us to go around the curve is called the **centripetal force** (see the Biomechanics section for more detail).

*Liam Williams tilting his skis so that they bend and are forced around the curve*

*Above and below, Deirdre (Dee) O'Neill's outside ski bends into reverse camber as the snow is compressed and resistance is built up*

## Movements that you can make

The movements that you make affect your balance in either a positive or negative way! To help you understand good and bad movements it is useful to look at the way that you move.

In other words there are three planes of movement – lateral, vertical and fore / aft, plus rotary movements that happen about an axis.

Lateral movement is more simply described as "side to side". You can move or lean your whole body to the inside of a turn and this is often referred to as inclination and allows you to edge your skis at the top of your turns. However, if you lean the body too far or too quickly to the inside (**banking**), you will end up either supported on your inside ski or worse still falling over.

As the turn shape develops you need to maintain control of your skis and keep effective balance against the outer ski of the turn. The hip, knee and ankle are all used to control the turn with the upper body reacting appropriately to help maintain balance.

*Colm Higgins showing an inclined body position at the top of the turn with his skis tilted onto their edges before the fall line*

*Derek Tate shows good control through the middle of the turn with the upper body reacting appropriately*

Vertical movements essentially involve extension and flexion of the legs. The execution of this requires a great deal of practice so that you learn to extend and flex the ankles, knees and hips in unison while maintaining a centred position. Timing is also important as this greatly effects how you control your skis. For example a quick extension will result in the skis being un-weighted at the end of the movement. Conversely, a gradual extension will help to maintain the control and grip of your skis against the snow.

Fore / aft movements are generally fairly subtle and are used to keep the skis working from tip to tail. These movements become more obvious when skiing bumps as the change in terrain requires fore / aft adjustment to help achieve ski to snow contact.

*Siobhain Duggan using appropriate fore / aft movement while skiing bumpy / variable snow*

Breaking movements down into three planes does in one sense help to simplify how you move, however it is important to understand that in a skilful skiing performance you combine these planes of movement. You do not simply move "up and down" to make your turns but rather combine lateral and vertical movements e.g. at the start of the new turn, as the hips move to the inside of the curve you extend your legs to apply pressure to your skis.

Rotary movements (about an axis) in layman's terms means "turning" and this could involve any part of the body. If for example I were to do a 360º spin, this would involve rotating the whole body. However, in general, when referring to rotary movements we are talking about turning our legs within our hip socket. You use this movement so that you can pivot your feet / skis (independently of the upper body) and this is an essential component for steering your skis which is described in more detail later is this segment.

## The process of Balancing

The reason for the term "balanc**ing**" rather than balance is to highlight that the process of balancing is not static. To maintain balance we continually make little adjustments. To highlight this point try standing on one foot and notice how you make subtle little movements in order to stay balanced. If you want to emphasise this even more then close your eyes.

Maintaining balance, while skiing is more complex than balancing while standing still. Balance in motion can be broken down into two distinct areas; Fore / aft (backwards & forwards) and lateral (side to side).

As you turn your skis you must maintain a relatively "centred" position so that you are stacked and balanced over your feet. Good **fore / aft balance** is achieved when you are supported by your bones through good skeletal alignment. To achieve this you need even flexion of your ankles, knees and hips. For example too much flexion in the knees and hips without ankle flex will quickly lead to very tired muscles.

*Colm demonstrates excellent skeletal alignment while snowplough turning and hence good fore / aft balancing*

**Lateral balance** can easily be compared to a cyclist going round a corner. If he / she leans the bicycle too far over in relation to the speed that they are travelling then they will fall over. In skiing, you tilt your skis and allow your body to lean to the inside of the turn. However, you must do this accurately so that you maintain effective balance against the outer ski of the turn.

*In this shot Colm combines excellent skeletal alignment with effective lateral balance*

If you want to test your skills at balancing then try turning using only the outer ski of the turn. This is best done initially on easier terrain. Try to keep your outer ski carving cleanly while keeping the inner ski lifted off the snow. You can get instant feedback (intrinsic) from this drill as to how well you are balancing both fore / aft and laterally. If your fore / aft balance is good then the lifted ski should be fairly level (not higher at the tip or tail!). And if your lateral balance is good you should be able to keep the inner ski lifted for the entire turn without any falling to the inside! Take a look at the next picture to see this exercise in action.

*In this shot Dee demonstrates perfect balance on the outer ski (with the carved track visible behind). The inner ski is lifted and level*

How to Steer your skis

I often describe skiing to my students in a very simplified way; i.e., there are just three things that you can do to your skis; Stand on them (pressure), tilt them (edging) and pivot them (rotation). However the complex part of this involves blending these three elements together. Lets' take a look at each of these elements…

**Pressure control** is often an area that causes confusion. As soon as you stand on a ski, you put weight on it and therefore exert some pressure. What you need to know is how to use pressure control within a turn and what effect gravity has on your skis. So when do you apply pressure to influence the turn and when do you control and manage pressure that is already there?

Take a look at the diagram below;

Diagram 1a

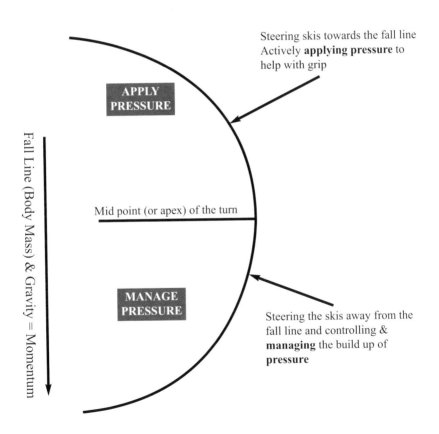

Steering skis towards the fall line Actively **applying pressure** to help with grip

APPLY PRESSURE

Fall Line (Body Mass) & Gravity = Momentum

Mid point (or apex) of the turn

MANAGE PRESSURE

Steering the skis away from the fall line and controlling & **managing** the build up of **pressure**

Through the first half of the turn your goal is to get your skis to grip. This can be done by balancing more against the outer ski of your turn either by bracing your leg or by actively stretching your leg and pressing the ski back into the snow thus creating more pressure.

In the second half of the turn you need to manage pressure that is already there due to turning your skis away from the fall line. As I have already mentioned a skier has momentum from sliding down the hill. Turning your skis across this line of momentum creates a build up of pressure that must be managed. This is done by allowing your legs to bend and absorb that pressure, which helps with maintaining good balance.

*Shona Tate, managing pressure, towards the end of the turn using good flexion of the legs*

There are a couple of good analogies which help with understanding how pressure control works; When in the gym using the leg press machine you extend or stretch your legs in order to lift the weight (actively applying pressure) while you bend your legs in order to lower the weight (manage the pressure).

Secondly, when you do a press up, you extend your arms to lift your body (apply pressure against the floor) and you bend your arms to lower your weight (manage the pressure).

One final important point with pressure control relates to the speed at which you make these stretching and bending movements of your legs. In other words, you need to distribute your movements to match the size and shape of your turn. If the timing of these movements is not matched to the size of the turn then you may lose grip or contact with the snow, which is fine if you want to un-weight your skis to bring them around more quickly as may be the case on a steep narrow slope.

**Edging** your skis involves tilting them at an angle so that the edges cut into the snow and help with grip. Assuming that you maintain balance and consequently effective pressure control then, the more you tilt your skis onto their edges, the tighter your turn will be. One of the most common phrases that I hear skiers say is, "I need to get more edge" when in reality what they need is to maintain effective balance against their outer ski so that the edge can grip. Edging movements can come from the lower leg (knees & ankles), from the hips or the whole body. At higher speeds the body comes further to the inside of the turn. The mistake that many recreational skiers make is that they edge their skis by moving their whole body inwards at lower speeds and consequently lose balance and grip.

You should aim to edge both skis equally as this promotes good balance and distribution of pressure between your skis.

*Derek illustrating equal edge tilt with daylight between the legs*

**Rotary movements** come from turning your legs within the hip socket. This results in pivoting the feet and skis. While both legs work independently of each other the goal is to get the inner leg and ski to copy the outer leg and ski so that there is simultaneous rotation (parallel skiing).

The easiest way to understand and become aware of leg rotation is to do a direct side slip, then pivot your feet & skis 180° so that you can side slip directly down the fall line facing the other direction. This should be done while keeping the upper body quiet and uninvolved.

Linking direct side slips together is often referred to as bracquage (or pivoting on the line) and is a skill practised by many good skiers and instructors to help focus on the rotary element of steering.

*Shona & Colm link*
*direct side slips together*
*(Bracquage*
*or pivoting on the line)*

If you can develop your ability and heighten your awareness of each of the steering elements then you will be in a much better position to **blend** these elements together to suit the terrain, your speed and the corridor that you wish to ski.

Skilful skiers have the ability to use all these elements in order to accurately steer their skis on whatever terrain the mountain throws at them.

Diagram 1b

# Basic Principles Model

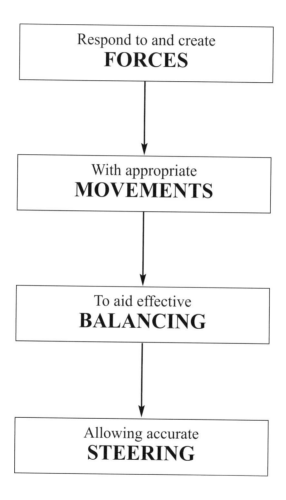

Respond to and create
**FORCES**

With appropriate
**MOVEMENTS**

To aid effective
**BALANCING**

Allowing accurate
**STEERING**

Respond to and create **Forces** with appropriate **Movements** to aid effective **Balancing** allowing accurate **Steering** of your skis.

Biomechanics is the language of movement. The purpose of this next section is to relate what I have already described in the previous pages about "Basic Principles" to Biomechanics thus giving you a deeper and sounder understanding of movement. University professor David Murrie's input is invaluable and helps validate the techniques that I have described.

## 1.2    Biomechanical principles
(by David Murrie)

*Shona demonstrates a plough turn showing good interaction with her equipment and the snow*

Biomechanics can give you the understanding of how you can effectively interact with your equipment and gravity (the primary cause of skiing movement) to create and control moving on skis.

Skiing can be thought of as a control and guidance activity, sliding down on a varying surface. The challenge is to play with gravity and the snow using your riding equipment so that you effect where and how you move (with positive results!). To enjoy the ride and ski more of the mountain, for more time, you need to acquire, by experience, better balancing whilst moving on your skis, plus effective change and control of your speed and direction. To change direction effectively you need to be able to change from using the ski(s) tilted on one side of you to the other; you need to change edge(s).

Your segmented body provides you with opportunities to use muscles and bones as levers to create and control movement. Holding ourselves rigid (with fear, inexperience or in a pose) is against the design of the body for movement. However, the freedom and opportunity to move that your non-rigid body provides, requires you to take time developing control of (excess) movement, and is a reason why the learning of sound movement patterns (technique) and core stability are important to skiers.

*Dynamic action showing freedom yet control!*

Since your connection to the snow is via your skis, and this is where the ground presses on you and you can press against the ground, the most important body segments to be aware of are the feet and legs operating effectively on the boot / binding to use the skis. As you can also press your ski poles against the ground then these actions can affect you're riding too – for good or bad.

## Posture and stance in skiing

Keep in mind most people do not have perfect posture or symmetry. Posture in skiing will be effective when you use your skeleton and muscles to best apply forces and manage the forces built up during skiing. Being well aligned, stacked (and angulated where necessary) helps you to have maximum effectiveness and safety. Generally speaking, the body is most efficient when in a tall stance where the spine and legs can transmit most of the forces through our bones with the minimum work for the supporting muscles.

## Mass, momentum & centre of gravity of the skier

Mass is a measure of how much matter there is in the skier. It indicates the amount of inertia or the resistance to change of motion. Momentum is a measure of how much motion there is. It is the product of the mass and the velocity. We can measure speed with a speed gun, but velocity is a measure of the speed and the direction of the skier. Momentum is a conserved quantity; it is constant until some force acts upon it. Larger or faster skiers have more momentum and need more force and strength to change direction or stop than smaller or slower skiers. The term `centre of gravity` refers to the simplified model of the body shape, representing this as a single point where the force of gravity can be assumed to be acting. However, keep in mind that other important forces are acting at the point of contact between the ski and the snow (see annotated photo of forces later in this section).

## Skier stability

Your stability can be manipulated and depends on five principles,
• the size of the base of support
• the height of the centre of gravity above the base
• the position  of the centre of gravity over the base
• the amount of grip you have
• the size of the mass

*Above Colm uses a wide stance and a low centre of gravity on steeper terrain, while on the right Siobhain skis a slalom turn on piste with a narrow stance and a higher centre of gravity*

Being centred over the base in a wide and flexed stance provides stability. Stability versus agility is in part a compromise choice. In general terms when you ski you use a wider and lower stance for stability and a narrower (but not necessarily the narrowest) stance for agility (would a goalkeeper stand for a penalty with feet together?).

## Forces in skiing

A force can be thought of as a push, pull, strain or exertion from one object on another. You are already familiar with the force of your weight as a consequence of gravity. Reaction force is a key concept for skiing; it is the response exerted by a second body on the first e.g. the snow slope against the ski / skier. Skiing is manipulating the ski / snow and pole / snow reaction forces. The reaction is equal in size but opposite in direction to the applied force. The more you press on the ground, the more reaction you will get, as long as the surface is resistive enough i.e. as long as you can compress the snow to support you or gain enough grip.

## Internal forces

These are the forces operating inside the skier system; inside the body, the boot, the binding and the skis. The skier can use muscles to press their feet (and thus skis) and press poles against the snow to create external forces on themselves. A key ski joint in the body is the hip with its accompanying internal and external rotator muscles for thigh turning.

*Maurice Duffy, IASI Trainer resisting the built up forces during a high speed GS turn*

*Photo by Sally Lee*

### The key skiing muscles

The tibialis anterior and the gastrocnemius are very active in the lower leg (for fore aft distribution) and all of the major muscles of the knee (the quadriceps and hamstrings) are key in knee flexion and extension during turns, especially in bumps. It is useful to know that the balance of the hamstrings to the quadriceps is a factor in protecting the anterior cruciate ligaments from excess tension and shear forces. Further, the gluteus and core muscles are used for stabilizing the pelvis and spine during turns. These muscles are the main ones that create internal forces to apply to the ski and effectively manage external forces.

### The concept of net external force

This is the overall force or the sum of all the forces on the body. In a schuss, for example in the Flying Kilometre, the effect of gravity will keep accelerating the skier down the slope until the air resistance becomes large enough to equal this external force and then the skier will stop accelerating, reaching what we call terminal velocity. At this point there is no net external force.

### Angular (circular) motion

This refers to rotation around a circular path and may be the path of the skis in a carved turn. During a carved turn there are ways you can influence angular motion by varying the size and direction of the reaction forces using pressure and edge control.

### Centripetal and centrifugal effects in ski turns

A net external force is needed to keep something moving in a circle or an arc and in a turn you sense the centrifugal effect of feeling thrown out. You create the centripetal force by the interaction of the ski with the snow, and inclining your centre of gravity inside the turn. If the net reaction force you generate is directed through your centre of gravity then you are balancing through the turn. The degree of inclination / angulation you need to adopt will depend on the speed and radius of the turn. Also, in simple terms, if the force providing the centripetal (centre seeking) effect is removed then the body will continue in a straight line. Visualise the release of a sling shot.

In skiing it is a little more complex, because your centre of gravity is away from where the ski forces are applied.

If you release your edges completely and remain balancing, you and your skis can slide straight at a tangent to the turn you were making. To make the transition smoothly into a new turn, you need to allow and manage lateral body movement whilst the ski continues to grip, creating a lateral toppling effect (crossover).

*Siobhain showing a smooth "**crossover**"*

In turning, as you accelerate down a slope, if you do not continue the inclination of your centre of gravity into the turn, then you will not maintain the centripetal force to keep you following the turn. Your centre of gravity can start to tip across the skis with the hips moving in the direction you next want to travel, instead of continuing around the turn. You need to smoothly change edges and engage the new turn with the skis gripping for you to settle against and prevent yourself from toppling over the skis completely. Then you can ride the new arc. It is a sensitive and learned feeling for balancing force and timing plus a willingness to trust and embrace gravity and the centrifugal effect. This can then produce flowing turns from a continuous, rhythmical, lateral rocking action (fine tuned by fore / aft pressure on the ski).

*Shane O'Connor in dynamic action managing the forces*
*Photo by Neil McQuoid, Racer Ready*

The line you take

In skiing, the movement direction is a result of the momentum and any new external force imparted to you from the reaction to your forces on the slope. In a turn, where you choose to be active on the arc has a direct result on the speed and the direction in which you propel yourself. Pushing against the ski that is uphill of the body, being active early in the arc, causes the reaction force direction to be more down the hill, while being active late in the arc, with the skis downhill of the skier, causes the reaction force direction to be more back up the hill.

*Sally Lee, IASI Level 4 showing active engagement of the skis above the fall line*

*Photo by Maurice Duffy*

*Shona uses the one ski carving drill to create active engagement above the fall line*

## Going faster

A change in velocity is referred to as acceleration (whether it is speed, direction or both that changes!) In ski racing there is little point in having the fastest speed gun reading if your line (direction) means that you are the slowest to the bottom, consequently direction and speed must be optimised. In skiing, velocity is largely affected by the direction in which we release the body's mass at the transition of a turn (when we change the reaction force). A common problem in performance skiing is when the skier releases too late and fails to harness the full benefits of acceleration, gravity and of the slope. This means the direction of movement is overly across or back up the hill as opposed to the usual goal of down the hill fast. With the intermediate skier a more common problem is too early a release and not finishing the turn.

## Impulse

Impulse is a combination of the amount of force exerted and the length of time the force is applied (F x t). While skiing you can use all sorts of impulses from short to long. Some are more effective for different snow types or terrain; the steepness of the slope and the desired outcome are all important factors when choosing the right kind of impulse to play with. For example carved, wide, open flowing GS turns where the skier carves a smooth arc from one turn to the next employ long duration force application (long impulse).

The skier taking a much more direct line and making short, perhaps even check or jump turns employs high impact movements, applying forces in short periods of time (short impulse).

Blending different impulses requires skill and precision and will enable you to respond seamlessly to changes in conditions and make smooth transitions between turns.

*Skiing bumps well means using a large range of flexion and extension to maximise the time and minimise the force of the impact*

### Moment of Inertia

Moment of Inertia is the spinning equivalent of body mass; it is the measure of the tendency to resist changes in spinning motion. This depends on both the size of the mass and how it is distributed in relation to the axis of rotation and is most relevant in aerials. Once airborne (e.g. Herman Maier – Nagano) the skier cannot exert a `net external force` to change the angular momentum that he / she has – there is nothing to press against to get a net external turning force! Unless you are doing the Flying Kilometre for example and go fast enough that dramatically increased air resistance can be used.

There are ways that the angular momentum you have can be managed though. During an aerial 1080 if you tuck in your arms and skis you will rotate faster (as this reduces your moment of inertia) whilst spreading them for landing will slow the rotation (as this change of mass distribution increases your 'moment of inertia').

The equipment

*A pair of modern shaped slalom skis with a lot of side cut (wide at the tip and tail and narrower under the foot / boot)*

**Skis** are designed to allow you to slide and turn on a bendable board, attached to your feet. Largely the design works by tilting an hour glass shaped flexible board that grips against the snow. The key mechanical features of a ski depend mainly upon its camber, torsional stiffness, side-cut, flex and taper angle.

The harder and rougher the surface and the faster and straighter you ski, the more the ski vibrates, giving intermittent contact with the snow. The innate camber of the ski acts as a spring to help keep the ski on the snow in a schuss and its core is constructed to dampen vibration reduce flex and increase durability. Additional dampers and stiffeners can also be included into the ski construction.

Modern skis are able to be much wider, especially at the tip, due to advances in torsional stiffness (resistance to twist about its long axis). A ski with high torsional stiffness is less prone to twist and lose edge grip in response to high loading. Conversely, a ski with low torsional stiffness is more forgiving and you are less likely to catch an edge. The wider ski means that for the same surface area underfoot the ski can be much shorter.

The greater side-cuts of modern skis again made feasible with materials and construction that resist twisting, allows the ski to flex more without losing grip and so turn and carve more easily and more sharply. This also allows carving of skis at slower speeds and with less skier strength.

Conversely, a high side-cut and soft flex can make a ski less stable in a straight line. The only way a ski with no side-cut (e.g. a spatula shaped ski) can flex into an arc is by displacing snow underneath it and thus the spatula shaped ski can be effective in deep powder.

A stiff ski tends to be better on ice, whereas a soft flexing ski is preferable in soft snow where the larger tip and tail help to bend the soft ski into an arc. The flex pattern of the ski will also affect its performance. Skis tend to be stiffest in the centre where they are thickest and a good ski for moguls would have a soft tip to absorb the initial impact and a stiff tail for braking.

The taper on a ski illustrates its curvature; the greater the angle, the smaller the turn radius. There are three varieties of taper; a wider shovel than tail, a narrower shovel than tail and equal shovel and tail. A wider shovel with high side-cut gives an easier turn initiation and support in deep soft snow whereas a wider tail would make the turn harder to initiate.

The way we control the skis is via the attachment of the skier to them i.e. the binding, and lifter plates and **boot**.

*A modern male ski boot in the binding with the lifter plates clearly visible under the toe and heel piece of the binding*

Problems occur when the skier has little awareness at the feet, or the flex or alignment of the foot and leg does not result in an effective line of force transmission. This can happen when the ski is not flat with the skier centred when standing normally on a horizontal surface. Forces and movements are then not transmitted effectively or efficiently. Higher, stiffer boots and lifter plates make alignment and degree of forward lean of the boot more important for optimizing performance. A customized orthotic foot-bed is necessary for most people for good boot fit and sound alignment.

In addition, the typically narrower heel, wider calf, wider hips and the more rearwards and lower position of the centre of gravity in women mean that different boot, binding and ski combinations are usually needed for optimizing women's performance.

*The women's boot (nearest) is lower to suit the different physiology as already mentioned*

For a strong arm-action, skiers are generally advised to have a **pole** length that creates no less than a right angle at the elbow. If the poles are really only to be used for poling (as in cross-country skiing) then longer poles are more effective for propulsion. Hence, longer poles may be useful for the start in ski racing but, for similar efficiency and effectiveness in soft snow and in bumps, shorter poles are needed.

*Shona uses slightly shorter poles which are appropriate for skiing bumps*

*Shona Tate skiing at Les Contamines Hauteluce*

*Photo by Alasdair Scobbie*

# Segment 2 – To Parallel Skiing

## 2.1 Core skier development – from beginner to parallel
(by Shona Tate & Derek Tate)

Now that you have read and understood segment 1 covering the "Basic Principles of Skiing" it is time to look at the stages that learners progress through on the road to becoming "parallel skiers". This segment is written so as to give advice to the ski instructor. However it is just as useful for the novice skier to read to help them understand their development on the road or should I say piste to parallel. Indeed as a keen recreational skier this segment will help you to gain a clearer understanding of how skiing works at slower speeds. We can all benefit from occasionally going back to basics. One of my favourite sayings is that "speed masks accuracy"!

An important point for instructors to take on board here is that your job is to teach the basic principles to your learners so that they continually develop their performance by learning to turn left and right more and more efficiently. The core skier development model simply provides you with a structure so that you can recognise where your learners are on the road to parallel skiing. You need to understand how the basic principles relate to these stages of development so that the movements that your learners make are efficient and effective.

What follows is a simple diagram of the stages of development within Core Skier Development with a brief description;

Diagram 2a

## Core Skier Development Stages Model

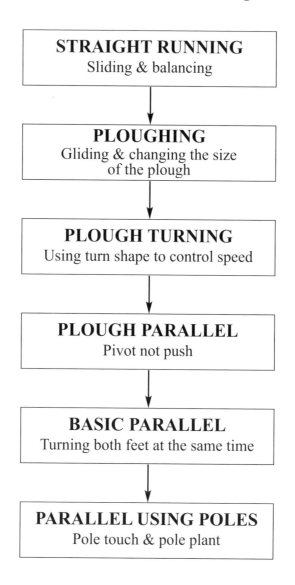

**STRAIGHT RUNNING**
Sliding & balancing

↓

**PLOUGHING**
Gliding & changing the size
of the plough

↓

**PLOUGH TURNING**
Using turn shape to control speed

↓

**PLOUGH PARALLEL**
Pivot not push

↓

**BASIC PARALLEL**
Turning both feet at the same time

↓

**PARALLEL USING POLES**
Pole touch & pole plant

Straight Running – sliding and balancing

The goal here is to develop confidence and balance while sliding. Instructor's must choose terrain carefully (ideally with a run out) as the control of speed at this point is determined by the terrain. Skiers should be encouraged to balance equally on both skis with the skis flat. A variety of drills can be practiced here to test balance but remember that the goal is to instil confidence. While it is inevitable that skiers will fall over while learning to ski, if beginners are continually falling over then the tasks or the terrain are too difficult. Instructors must take responsibility for ensuring that this does not happen.

*Posture should be balanced and aligned over the feet with light flexion in the ankles, knees and hips. Skis should be flat on the snow*

Ploughing – gliding and changing the size of the plough

This is where the skier learns to control speed. However choice of terrain is once again crucial at this stage. If the gradient is too steep then the skier will need to make a large plough shape which will result in poor posture and a defensive approach to skiing.

Remember that "Practice makes permanent", while "Correct practice makes perfect".

The movements required to go from a straight run to a plough are turning of both legs / feet, while displacing the feet slightly wider than the hips. This draws the tips of the skis closer while moving the tails of the skis wider. You need to encourage "rotation" under the foot rather than pushing the tails out! Again a variety of tasks can be practiced here but the goal is to develop a stable gliding plough position on easy terrain. Time spent achieving this is time well spent as turning will be much easier.

*Plough gliding on easy terrain. Tips are drawn together as tails move apart. Rotation happens under the foot. The size of the plough is small promoting good posture*

Plough Turning – Using turn shape to control speed

A good stance has now been created over the skis to help maintain balance while sliding over the slippery surface and now it is time to learn how to make turns so that the skier can move down a slope keeping control of both direction and the rate of descent.

It is important to maintain the width of the plough (feet slightly wider than the hips) as the skis start to change direction. Imagine the plough as an arrowhead pointing in the direction the skier wishes to travel. Starting in a gliding plough, directly down the fall line to give slight motion, gently rotate both skis (arrowhead) to the left. On a slight slope the skis will take the skier to the left, keeping a little momentum (before the skis come to a stop) rotate the feet back to centre (fall line) and to go to the right continue to rotate the feet in that direction. This is the first principal of linking turns.

Once the skis can be changed confidently in both directions it is time to move to a slightly steeper slope to practice the same task but allowing the outside ski to create a natural edge against the snow.

To develop plough turns so that the skier can explore more of the beginners' area safely your learners need to add in some movement from their ankles, knees & hip joints to help the accuracy of the plough turns.

*Plough turning sequence showing initiation through to completion of turn*

When rotating towards the fall line the hips should be progressively **stretched** away from the feet by making the legs long (keeping hips above the feet at all times). As rotation happens through the turn, progressively shorten the legs (bending) to a point where there is a feeling of being balanced well against the outside ski with the skis having been turned sufficiently around the arc. At this point the stretch starts to initiate the next change of direction (back to centre). These movements need to be timed accurately to match the turn shape that the skier is trying to achieve (C shape), thus continuous stretching and bending movement with the legs and rotation of the legs / feet. The complex aspect here is the ability to blend more than one movement together at the same time e.g. stretch & rotate, bend & rotate.

An important fundamental point here is that as the plough turner develops their skill at turning the overall size of the plough shape will reduce with the shape of the turn being a crucial element in the control of speed. However for any given set of turns the plough shape will always remain the same size thus encouraging the turning of both feet and avoiding any lateral pushing movements.

Plough Parallel – pivot not push

Now that the skier has learned to steer the skis accurately in both directions and can keep control of the descent down the hill by the line that is taken, they can be taken a step closer to becoming a parallel skier (which is what every beginner skier strives to be able to achieve – instructors should not forget that!).

Moving onto the next level of slope (blue / easy red) will give the skier more momentum and the skis will travel more easily around the arc. When the management of the build up of pressure, in the second half of the turn, has been achieved the inside leg / foot can then be rotated more than previously. Initially the tips of the skis keep pointing towards each other until safely passed the fall line. At that point separate the inner tip from the outer tip (tips apart) to let the skis become parallel, finishing the arc with a controlled parallel skid.

Diagram 2b

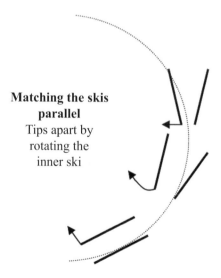

**Matching the skis parallel**
Tips apart by rotating the inner ski

As long as the terrain does not become steeper or more variable (bumps / chopped up soft snow / slush) the skier will become competent quite quickly at plough parallel. The snow and gradient of the slope will help the inside ski rotate earlier & earlier around the turn. With practice the skier will soon be matching the skis parallel from the fall line.

> *It is important that the skier is kept in their comfort zone and on familiar terrain so that this development can take place. If the skier is stressed by any of the above they will initially resist matching the skis and increase the size of their plough shape to "keep the brakes on!"

The choice of the word "matching" is very important as the goal is to allow the inside ski to copy the outside one so that both skis are steered in a curve. The distance between the feet in a good plough turn and a plough parallel should not be significantly different. The mistake that many skiers make at this stage is to focus too much on bringing the inner ski parallel, often by sliding it in closer or lifting it in followed by a traverse! The result of this is poor turn shape which creates a block in the skiers' ability to steer both skis parallel.

As skiers and teachers it is better if you can focus on developing the correct movement patterns rather than trying to improve a specific manoeuvre such as plough parallel.

> **Teach the basic principles and improve the ability to turn left & right rather than teaching the individual turning stages of core skier development.**

We have looked quite closely at how the skis are matched and steered parallel but it is equally important that the initiation of the turn is such that it is helping the skier to develop towards parallel. Therefore to start the next turn the legs are stretched as before, while the outer foot / ski is pivoted to make a small plough, bringing the outer tip closer to the inner tip (tips together).

Diagram 2c

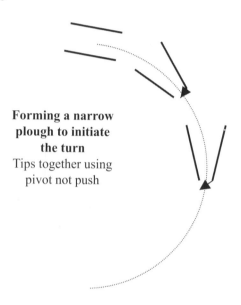

**Forming a narrow plough to initiate the turn**
Tips together using pivot not push

Again it is crucially important that the plough size remains small so that the skier's hips flow into the turn. Pushing the foot out would cause breaking and create a blockage in the development towards parallel.

### Remember PNP – Pivot not Push!

So we can to an extent simplify the movements in plough parallel as "tips together, tips apart". As the skier improves the duration of the plough will reduce NOT the size of the plough.

Basic Parallel – turning both feet at the same time

With plough parallel most skiers can travel safely around 80% of the pisted mountain. To get them through that next 20% requires patience from both instructor and pupil alike.

All the previously learned skills need to be practiced with revision on balance, steering and controlled skidding. The key factors that contribute to "parallel" throughout the turn are increased speed around the curve and an increase in the gradient (but not necessarily both at the same time!) This allows the skier to become effectively balanced against the outer ski earlier and earlier thus making it easier for the inner ski to copy.

This is also the time that the "crossover" effect is felt and becomes more evident (as can be seen in the photo sequence below). This is where the hips come forward and across the feet as the edges of the skis are changed. In reality this movement is developed in plough parallel provided the movement pattern is correct (as described earlier).

The definition of a parallel turn is when the distance between the tips and the tails remains the same for the whole turn. Both legs / feet are rotated simultaneously and eventually both edges are changed at the same time with the feet about hip width apart. If not challenged by terrain the average skier will naturally progress into parallel turns but if the gradient of the slope is too steep control will be lost very quickly!

Parallel using Poles – pole touch & pole plant

To help with timing of the turns and the coordinating of all the movements a pole plant can be introduced. Initially lightly touching the snow on the inside of the turn as the stretch is carried out (change of edges) and giving the skier commitment to making the turn. The pole touch should be by a rotation of the wrist (hands already forwards from the waist) and not a whole upper body swing.

When the skier is ready to move onto steeper slopes and use shorter radius turns the **pole plant** becomes more important. It signals the initiation of the turn and gives an extra point of balance. The pole also gives feedback from the snow – hard packed / soft / powder / hollow / not there at all! This feedback gives additional information that will help you make any adjustments required to complete the turn successfully and in control.

*Derek shows a complete parallel turn using a pole touch to help the timing and co-ordination of the movements and the changing of the edges*

## 2.2    Skidding & Carving

Definitions;

A ski can be said to be carved when the path of the tip and the tail are the same. Conversely a ski is skidded when the tail washes out to the side.

The track left by a ski that is carved is very thin and a good carved turn will leave two tracks in the snow rather like railway lines (as can be seen in the photo below).

The track left by a skidded turn will be fatter as the ski(s) are moving sideways and forwards around the curve (as can be seen in the next diagram 2d).

Diagram 2d

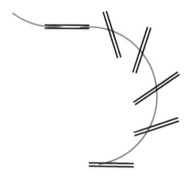

Good skidding and bad skidding;

Many people advocate that skidding is bad! This is a misconception as skidding is an essential skill if you want to be able to effectively ski the whole mountain. There is however such a thing as good skidding and bad skidding. The difference between the two was summed up recently by an instructor who was participating in a staff training session that I was running when he said PNP. As stated earlier in this segment this stands for "Pivot not Push".

Side slipping is an essential skill for developing control, balance and more importantly good skidding. Many skiers struggle once a slope becomes icy and the common stated solution is that "I need to get more edge". However what often happens is that the skier edges the skis by leaning the whole body into the hill and consequently loses balance and control as the skis slide out from underneath them (bad skidding). By developing your side slipping skills you learn to slide and therefore skid in balance. The next stage is to develop edge control by tilting the skis onto their edges using a gentle rolling of the feet towards the hill.

So the next time you come across an icy slope edge less initially so that you maintain balance and slide in control. Then think about edging from the feet up!

*Tracks that dreams are made of!*
*These tracks are made using rotation of the legs to blend rotation through the curve (good skidding rather than bad skidding)*

# Record of Notes, Thoughts & Ideas

*Robbie Fenlon in action in Les Contamines Hauteluce*
*Photo by Alasdair Scobbie*

# Segment 3 – All Mountain Skiing

## 3.1　Performance on Piste
　　　　(by Shona Tate)

In this book so far we have identified the individual aspects of how to balance on skis while moving over the snow and how to use the many different movements to make the skis work for you.

Skiing is about constantly moving, using your equipment effectively to support you and your body positioning to help you maintain balance on your skis. Whether the terrain is flat or variable you are always moving and making adjustments to keep your centre in an efficient place to achieve the required outcome.

The biomechanics section has explored these movements and forces in great depth so we need to now look at how to put all of this information / skill together to produce the outcome – **Flowing Linked Turns!**

I will cover 3 main areas:
Technical Performance (input movements)
Tactical Decisions (output focus)
Flowing Linked Turns (skilful performance)

Technical Performance (input movements)

As you practice skiing and developing your performance, your skill level and accuracy will improve. This will then enable you to ski on piste using different types and shapes of turns and to control your speed both round the arcs and in your descent of the run.

Different types of turns would either be with skidding (good rather than bad skidding!) or you would purely carve your turns.

"Skiing is about constantly moving, you use your equipment(1) effectively to support you and your body positioning to help you maintain balance on your skis(2)".

**How the shape of the skis help you to turn** (1)
The hour glass shape of the skis helps you to form the shape of an arc in the snow. This is achieved by tilting the skis onto their parallel edges and applying the appropriate pressure.

The shape of the ski and its' torsional stiffness will determine the minimum radius that you can achieve (most skis will have this figure written on them); this is how tight you could possibly make a turn without rotating the skis underneath you. You need to actively apply pressure and edge tilt (angle) to work the skis throughout the whole turn in order to influence the shape of the curve.

**Carving** - this can also be referred to as a small steering angle, the tail of the ski follows the line of the tip of the ski.
**Skidding** - if you want to produce a skidded turn you would increase the steering angle (rotate the skis during the turn and blend all the steering elements appropriately).

**Diagram 3a**

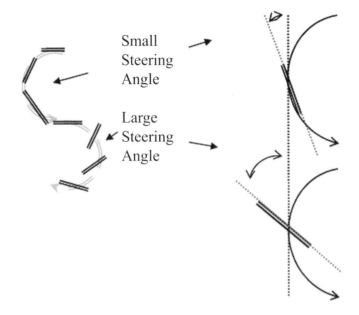

Small Steering Angle

Large Steering Angle

**Centre of Gravity** (2)

As your centre of gravity moves round the arc, momentum is built up (by gravity itself), the greater the speed, the greater the momentum. With the upper body you must think of facing it in the direction of travel. If you are travelling a long way round the arc (from the fall line) the upper body will face slightly to the outside of the arc to keep momentum in the direction of travel (diagram 3b).

**Diagram 3b**

The centre of gravity itself (solid line) however will move along a line just inside the arc of the skis (parallel lines). As you see in diagram 3c the solid line is your centre point which crosses over your skis as the skis change edges from one turn to the next.

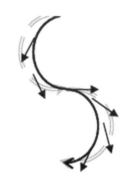

**Diagram 3c**

This is highlighted in the photograph, here you can see the whole body picture with the intersection of the white lines (on hips) showing the path of the racers centre in relation to the line of the skis.

This photograph also shows you how the racer deals with the forces as he makes the cleanest and fastest path around the pole.

*Shane O'Connor*
*Photo by Neil McQuoid,*
*Racer Ready*

Key Points
• feet hip width apart for strong solid platform
• equal edge angle created with parallel shins
• inclination of body towards the centre of the turn to create edge angle early and before the fall line
• early signs of angulation of the body to manage the centrifugal effect and maintain efficient balance

To produce skilful, accurate turns at higher speeds and on steeper gradients we must consider:

The speed and the degree that you;
1. Engage / disengage the edges of the skis
2. Rotate your skis across the fall line
3. Use pressure management

At what point of the turn you do the above and whether you use rotation or not will enable you to change the shape of your turns. *Not forgetting all the other basic principles we have discussed previously, but implementing them with accuracy.

By saying "good skidding rather than bad skidding" we are referring to a steered turn with the blending of all the steering elements (pressure / edge / rotation) around the arc to produce the "grip" you require on that chosen part of the piste while controlling your speed.

*"Grip"* – *the dictionary describes grip as – "firm hold, grasping power, mastery, grasp or hold tightly"*
To me I think of being in charge of how far down the slope I will travel when making my turn (any drift or not) and the speed at which I want to travel around that turn.
"What am I trying to achieve?"

## a) Short turns (skidding)

A racer, especially a slalom racer will not use skidding in his / her run unless they make a mistake or perhaps lose grip on the ice causing them to drop out of the racing line for the next gate. They are trying to achieve a descent down a dictated route in the quickest time possible. They do not wish to slow down their forwards momentum so they will not use the rotation element of steering unless necessary to make a correction and achieve that next gate. The racer must use the shape of the skis and coordinate the movements to be able to accelerate around the arc, while maintaining balance and keeping the flow from one turn to the other without any pauses in speed.

However as **you** ski down a piste you have more freedom than the racer and for most of us the aim is not to descend the run as quickly as possible in the same way as the racer. It requires an immense degree of skill to be able to carve short turns on steeper gradient and maintain control of speed. This is something you can strive towards, but build up to it.

You should aim to be in control of your skis & body and enjoy the descent – to achieve this you need to be very skilful on your skis (good at maintaining balance, agile, responsive and reactive to the snow textures and gradient). A series of linked short turns requires you to be able to quicken up all the movements that you have already learned and be able to use them in quick succession.

Key points;

- your edges must change simultaneously and your shins should be as parallel as possible to help this to happen
- allow upper and lower body separation (legs and feet rotate underneath you without the upper body turning all the way round at the same time), letting the feet initiate the movement. Keep your hips closer to the fall line but not so rigid that you restrict the turn and lose versatility.  (You still need to feel a connection with the hips; if not you might fall into the area where you counter rotate.  Here the hips get pushed into an opposite direction to the feet; the hips are then too rotated away from the direction of travel. The skier is unable to reconnect them quickly enough and you end up out of balance. Perhaps you may have felt this before!)
- engage the edge at or before the fall line
- effective use of fore & aft movement
- keep the turns flowing into each other with co-ordinated movements
- maintain effective balance over your skis throughout

### b)  High speed carving (longer radius turns)

What words could you use to describe the picture you have in your head of the perfect high speed, long carved turns on a smooth wide open piste?

Clean, pure, strong, powerful, stable, two clear parallel lines left in the snow……to name just a few.

Carving is using the skis shape and structure to cut through the surface in a forwards movement around the arc (previously mentioned in Segment 2.2).

To be able to ski illustrating the descriptive words and phrases and to be successful in the task, you need to have equipment that will help you to achieve it safely. As you are relying on stability at higher speeds you need equipment that will support you as you play with the forces. Stiffer skis will give you a stronger platform to balance against as you are accelerated around the turn and likewise a boot that has good lateral control will help you to hold the ski on edge (grip) at greater speeds and influence the shape of the turn and the line that you take down the hill (see segment 1.2 Equipment).

When you are very clear on the biomechanical principles (section 1.2) you will begin to understand the implications of travelling further round the arc and at higher speeds. You have a lot of forces to deal with accurately, otherwise the consequences are that your upper body & equipment (skis) get thrown in the opposite direction as you release from one turn to the next!

Movements that you need to make –

(Phases - initiation, midpoint, settling)

Crossover;

At the **initiation** of the turn you need to start to stretch the legs simultaneously and with a forwards motion let the hips come up & over the feet towards the inside of the new turn (**crossover & inclination**). With this lateral movement the skis roll from top edges over through flat skis to the new turning edges. This projection of the body in the direction of the future turn is important as you want to bring the hips into the fall line (letting the outside ski catch up with the new inside one). For example, at this point the racer is balanced effectively with the momentum of the turn. You will now be in the **midpoint** (apex) of the turn.

This next point is extremely important; to keep the skis running along their edges (not rotating the feet) you must now add angulation. Angulation (breaking at the hip and / or lower legs) compliments the earlier creation of inclination. In that phase you set the skis onto their edges with extended legs and level shoulders and now angulation will help you to maintain edge grip when the forces build up in the next part of the turn. To be strong and powerful you need to maintain a long outside leg until you are ready to exit that turn. *The amount of angulation created should be appropriate to the speed and radius of the turn.

In the last phase of the turn flex the legs slightly and slowly to **settle** over the skis managing the build up of pressure and then stretch again to initiate the next turn.

When releasing from one turn to the next you must be careful not to do this too quickly as there is a risk that you will be catapulted by the forces that were carrying you around the previous turn. This situation would feel like your skis being "pinged" and leaving the snow as your body wants to keep going around that last arc.

**Diagram 3d**

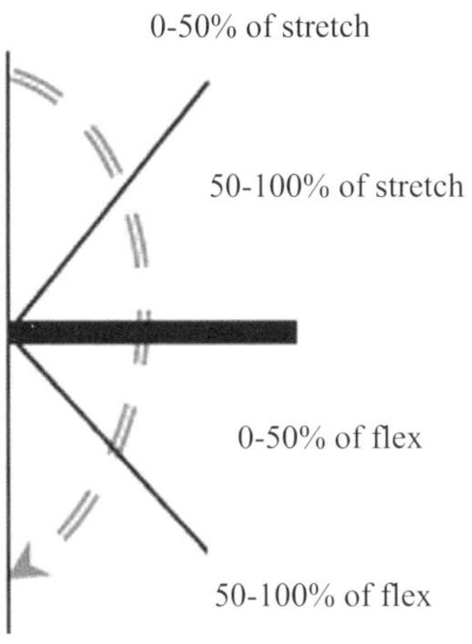

0-50% of stretch

50-100% of stretch

0-50% of flex

50-100% of flex

**Blending appropriate rate and range of movement**

If you split the arc of a turn into segments (I have used 4) from where the arc crosses the fall line it will help you to picture the progressive stretch & flex movements, appropriate to the turn to help produce a consistent shaped flowing arc.

*Shane O'Connor representing Ireland at the 2003 World
Championships in St. Moritz, Switzerland*

*Photo courtesy of the Croatian Team*

Key points;
- carving cleanly on both skis
- inclining at the top of the turn and angulating appropriately for the speed that has been built up
- ability to influence the line you take, while maintaining the carve
- keep the turns flowing into each other with co-ordinated movements (release from one turn to the next)
- maintain effective balance over your skis throughout

Cross under;

As with the above, (crossover), you can change the edges simultaneously by using more of a "cross under" effect. This is maintaining a low position with the body (through the end of the turn) and retracting the feet back under the path of the body to change edges for the new turn. A crossover tends to be used to make a progressive edge change while the cross under can be used when you wish to make a quick edge change. In reality most skiers change edge using a blend of these two methods i.e. as the hips cross over the feet, the feet travel under the body!

Tactical Decisions (output focus)

### a) Gradient & terrain

You need to decide the terrain and gradient of the slope you wish to use. This will determine the shape of the turns that you choose. For example; if you want to do short turns on a steep slope (to keep control) in a narrow corridor (as if in a couloir) you will require more rotation across the fall line with an edge check and strong pole plant to maintain control and balance.

It would be inappropriate to think that you can ski all terrain and gradients the same way; you may even mix and match the type of turns that you use down a run. This flexibility shows that you are skilled at what you can do and can adapt to the surface that you are on to make skiing fun and lively not robotic and static. The nature of body mechanics allows you to be flexible in your stance, as you change direction and travel over undulating terrain you will be able to produce that inspiring performance!

Being able to train yourself to look ahead and picture the next couple of turns is extremely important, you should have already mentally completed the turn you are currently on by the time your skis are reaching the fall line and know what type and what the size the next turn will be (see segment 4.2 Psychology & Skiing Performance).

## b) Turn shape & corridors

Moving on from gradient & terrain we can look further at the different turn shapes that you can achieve;

For example; you can make round turns where you leave a C shape in the snow (linking into S shapes) or you can make J shape turns where you have quicker movements (sudden rotation then putting edge tilt on very quickly to a high angle) in the second half of the turn.

The better you become the more you can use the S shape turns and the length of the arc to help control your speed (faster / slower / consistent). As the diagrams below show you can use different arcs (how far you travel round the arc past the fall line, before releasing from that turn) & radius (relating to how big the circle would be) for your turns.

**Diagram 3e**

• **Turn Radius & Arc**

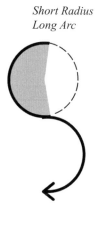

*Short Radius*
*Long Arc*

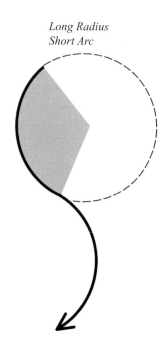

*Long Radius*
*Short Arc*

As mentioned previously you want to be able to use variety and versatility in your chosen line on your chosen gradient and terrain. To help you develop your skill at using and defining turn sizes you can use corridors to work within. As seen in diagram 3e (long radius, short arc), the earlier you release from one turn to the next the shorter the arc length and therefore your turns will be more direct down the fall line. On steep gradient this would produce a much faster descent than using the first turn (short radius, long arc).

Different corridors that can be used to develop your skills;

**Diagram 3f**

• **Corridors**

i) short radius / long arc = 5 turns   ii) long radius / short arc = 3 turns

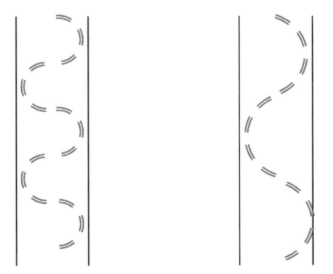

These 2 corridors are the same size but they show different arc length turns to show how many turns can be fitted in on the same length of pitch. To mark the corridor you can use; markers / cones / slalom poles / mat widths or piste machine tracks.

## Diagram 3g

### • Funnel

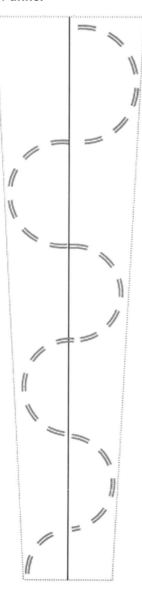

With the funnel the turns initially start wider and then become narrower as you move further down the hill. This is a very good test of blending the steering elements appropriately.

## Diagram 3h

- **Hour glass**

Diagram 3h is a variation of the funnel. At the top of the hour glass the turns are wider and as you move to the middle the turns tighten up becoming narrower then opening out to wider again at the bottom of the hour glass.

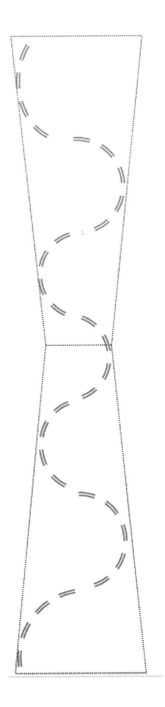

**Diagram 3i**

• **Forest**

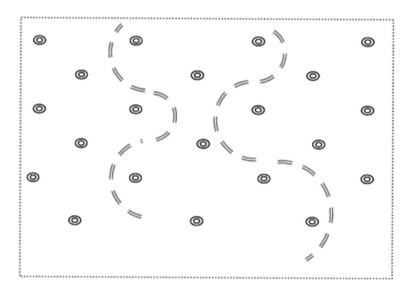

A forest of markers can be used to show versatility by changing each turn. The task on the left is to turn around one marker at a time, the task on the right is to make the first 2 turns on one marker each and then the next turn round 2 markers. You could also use colours to identify the skier's route down the forest (e.g. red / blue / red / blue).

### c) Control of speed

As a skier travels down any slope they pick up some speed, the steeper the gradient and the slippier the surface the faster the skis will slide.

You need to decide how fast you want to make your descent down the piste (while maintaining control & safety!). And then set yourself the task of what shape and size of turn you will use and in what corridor. This goal must be within the boundaries of your ability on such a piste. As also mentioned in the section before you can use shorter arcs to let the skis stay closer to the fall line and thus increase in speed or lengthen the arc to come further round the circle almost back up the hill again to take off the speed at the end of the turn.

Another way of slowing down is of course by rotating the feet and skis to create a skid or braking action.

You can choose to;
• Maintain a consistent speed
• Descend quickly
• Descend slowly

The movements that you make will influence these 3 speeds. Quick movements will make your skis react and turn quicker, slow movements will let the skis react more slowly. To maintain a consistent speed you need to be able to read the terrain and blend fast & slow movements to maintain the same speed of descent.

Flowing Linked Turns (skilful performance)

Achieving flowing linked turns is very much about combining technique and tactics to produce a skilful outcome.

This section is about adding some "mojo" to your skiing!

### a) Rhythm

Without rhythm your turns will be disjointed and stand alone from each other, rhythm gives you timing and precision to your movements.  It helps you commit to the next turn when the terrain or gradient becomes challenging (rather than traversing the slope saying – I'll turn here… no here…no here…until you simply have no more slope left and you have to do something!).

Rhythm can be developed by using many different activities, such as;

• Timing of your pole plant and co-ordinating your movements
   with this
• Counting as you plant each pole, on each turn (1-2, 1-2)
• Singing a rhyme / song to yourself
• Using a specific corridor so that the turns are consistent

## b) Fluency

Once you have developed rhythm within all turn shapes, on all terrain and gradients you will start to feel (and the audience will see) that your turns have some flow. **Flow** can be described as the icing on the cake, all the ingredients have been baked together and bonded well, now the outside layer is put on and the cake looks mouth watering! The bonding part is very important, if some of the ingredients do not bond then the cake shows flaws and it can crumble into pieces. To relate this to your linked turns, your movements will be seen as individual segments, put together in succession, these can come across as being robotic or erratic movements with pauses between each segment. Often looking like a huge amount of energy used for a very poor outcome. If you show flow in your turns the joins from one segment to the other would be seamless and look effortless both mentally & physically.

## c) Skiing with skill (automatic adjustments)

Ready for the cake decorations, that awe inspiring performance that we talked about earlier. The skis are used with versatility & flair, the skier uses the terrain to show skill and playfulness. There is no thought process other than reading and feeling for the terrain, the movements that the skier makes are autonomous, they happen automatically!

In conclusion, working on your performance on piste as described will very much help with your preparations for skiing bumps and the backcountry.

## 3.2 Bumps

*Awe inspiring; skiing bumps showing flair*

Skiing bumps (moguls) is one of the most exciting challenges that the mountain can throw at you. They challenge every aspect of your ability, testing your technique, your tactics, your fitness and your mental strength. Skiing the bumps well will give a great sense of achievement and will help with the development of your all round skills for coping with skiing the whole mountain.

To help with understanding how to ski the bumps this part of segment three has been divided up as follows;
- Common problems (or blockages to effective performance)
- Key skills that need to be developed
- Additional aspects that require consideration

Common problems

a) Breaking forward from the waist

This is one of the most common problems and is caused by the constantly changing terrain. If you allow yourself to fold forward from the waist your balance will be severely compromised and your ability to bend your legs will be reduced. To prevent this you need to focus on the placement of your feet allowing them to move ahead of you as you ski towards the bump. This will allow the legs to bend & absorb the bumps while keeping a strong core and upright upper body. To help understand this movement try the following off skis; from an upright standing position lift one leg using the hip and knee, so that your foot is out in front of you (a little like the preparation for a front kick in karate). Then, bend forward from your waist and try the same movement! You should notice that the range of available movement has now been severely reduced.

b) Too wide a stance

During the 90s there was a revolution in ski design and much of our focus turned to piste skiing and "carving". Having spent the 80s trying to keep our stance as close as possible the 90s became a time when a wide stance was more fashionable! However your "stance" needs to be appropriate for the terrain that you are skiing rather than trying to adhere to some in vogue fashion!

Bumps require a slightly closer stance simply because it is a more efficient way to negotiate the terrain. Too wide a stance can lead to one foot being in a trough while the other is on the bump which in turn will challenge your balance even more!

It is also a question of stability versus agility? Carving on piste at higher speeds requires a good base of support (wider stance) and an ability to use bigger edge angles. Bumps require quick movements with the ability to ski the fall line and therefore a narrower stance for agility.

*Derek uses a narrow stance to promote agility in the bumps*

*Photo by Sally Lee*

c) Arms too wide with elbows in

If your arm carriage is too wide it can lead to problems with over rotation of the upper body. Pole planting is essential for timing and support when skiing bumps. Many skiers plant their pole and then allow their hand / arm to be dragged behind them which leads to body rotation and loss of balance. It is important therefore to use efficient movement of your wrist when planting your poles with a focus on planting the tip of the pole slightly ahead of your hand, at an angle rather than straight up and down. Then focus on keeping that hand in your peripheral vision as the hand goes past where the pole was planted.

Also if you ski with your elbows in then this can block your body's ability to move freely. Keeping your hands a little closer and in vision, with the elbows out will help to cure this problem.

Key skills that need to be developed

a) Leg absorption

This is probably the skill that people find most difficult to learn. We need a big range of movement in our legs to help absorb and check our speed.

A good way to begin developing this skill is to traverse the bumps field and use your legs like shock absorbers (remember the description from earlier as you do this). Then link these traverses together as you make your way down the mogul field. Gradually you can reduce the length of the traverse until eventually you start to link one turn into the next. To add variety to this practice and increase the challenge, adjust the angle of the traverse (steeper) so that you have to deal with more speed. The leg absorption movements will need to happen much more quickly and this is similar to what you will experience in an attacking fall line bump run.

Next you should practice compression turns on the piste; this involves mimicking the movements required in bumps while on a smooth piste. Towards the end of the curve you absorb and bend your legs (using mainly the knees and hips as mentioned earlier), allowing your feet to go ahead of you slightly, then change edge in this low position and stretch your legs into the next curve.

Practicing this on piste may seem a little strange and will place you in a slightly "sitting back" position but when you transfer this to bumpy terrain it is an appropriate movement for maintaining balance as the terrain changes.

*Derek shows good leg absorption with the feet going slightly ahead*

b) Stretching the legs

Developing good absorption is essential but to avoid getting caught in the back seat you need to respond to the change in terrain as you come over or around the bump. Essentially this involves pushing the tips of your skis down as you stretch your legs in order to maintain as much snow contact as possible. As you reach the crest of the bump it is useful to think about pulling your feet back underneath you. This will help to engage the front of your skis as you begin to stretch your legs and will ensure that you don't get left behind! Focus on making this movement with both skis as quite often skiers lift the front of the inside ski which again causes problems with balance and pressure control.

Bending and stretching of the legs in bumps allows you to use good fore / aft pressure control. As you bend and absorb with the legs you allow the pressure to move towards the tails of the skis. And then as you stretch your legs and push the tips down you move the pressure towards the front of the skis.

*In this shot Derek shows good stretching of the legs with the tips being pushed down*

c) Leg rotation

It is not enough to simply bend and stretch your legs. You also need very good leg rotational skills. This has been discussed earlier in the book in the basic principles segment and can be developed with drills like "pivoting on the line".

What is important to appreciate here is that you need to develop the active movement of turning your legs independently of your upper body, which should remain relatively passive. This produces what we call rotational separation.

*In the sequence opposite Shona shows active leg rotation independent of the upper body*

Apart from drills like pivoting on the line it is a good idea to practice lots of short turn drills on piste, keeping a narrow corridor and maintaining good control of speed. You can then build in a number of different rotational separation drills to help keep the upper body passive and uninvolved. Again I stress here that the goal is not so much to keep the upper body facing down the fall line (although this may be the result) so much as to actively turn your legs independently of the upper body.

Once you can achieve controlled rotary short turns on piste you can then take this practice into some small bumps. This is when side slipping again becomes such a useful skill as you can use it between turns (rotation of the legs) to control your speed by sliding down the back of the bump. This will give you a lot of confidence in negotiating this challenging terrain. Gradually you can build in greater stretching of the legs and use more of a steered arc, as described earlier, with bending and stretching movements.

## Additional aspects that require consideration

### a) Finding the right line

Should you ski the ruts? Should you ski over the bumps? Or should you do a mixture of the two? To be honest it doesn't really matter. If you develop the skills that I have already discussed you will be able to tackle the bumps in different ways. The gradient and the quality of the skiers who made the bumps will influence how easy the line is to find. For some bumps the line will be irregular and you will need to be adaptable for others the line will be more obvious and rhythmical. What is essential is that you look ahead. It is a good idea to pause at the top of each run and look and see where you are going to place your skis as if you were descending some steep steps.

b) Playing with terrain

It is worth noting that skiing bumps is not just about skiing the fall line or staying in a big rut line, it is also about playing with and using the terrain. The ability to change your line, change your speed, increase the number of turns or even take a little air all contribute to a more exciting, free and skilful performance.

*Shona and Derek playing with the terrain at les Grands Montets in Argentière*

c) Attack – mentally & physically

Ultimately skiing bumps requires commitment and a positive mental approach. Of course you can ski them slowly and this in itself requires great skill and precision. However to ski the fall line and take on the bigger bumps you need more rather than less! More range of movement, more vision to see further ahead and an attitude that says, "I'm going to eat up these bumps".

*Attacking the bumps*

### 3.3.1  Off Piste & Backcountry
(by Derek Tate)

When people think of off piste they tend to imagine those perfect untouched slopes of virgin powder, with a clear blue sky, breathtaking scenery and wall to wall sunshine! Well occasionally it does happen and I was lucky enough to enjoy just such a day last season while skiing the Vallée Blanche in Chamonix (see the back page photo and below). However in reality when referring to off piste, we include every kind of snow condition that you may experience once you venture from the marked, machine groomed runs. In reality a more appropriate name for this is variable conditions. To become a real all mountain skier you need to be able to tackle the variable snow conditions that you will find away from the piste in the backcountry.

*Liam enjoys a perfect day on la Vallée Blanche*

Before Robbie covers the wider aspects of backcountry skiing lets take a look at the techniques and tactics required to tackle these variable snow conditions.

One of the greatest challenges of off piste skiing is the wide range of snow types that you will encounter and these can include; deep untracked snow which could range from champagne powder to densely packed wind blown snow, breakable crust where the top layer of the snow appears to hold you but then breaks through, chopped up tracked snow which has not yet been skied enough to make bumps. These are just a few examples of what you may experience!!

To help with understanding how to ski the backcountry this part of segment three has been divided up as follows;
• Deeper snow
• Chopped up tracked snow
• Steeper slopes

Deeper snow

So lets take a closer look at skiing deeper snow (whatever its' consistency) and cover one of the most common myths that I regularly hear people saying, "you need to sit back to ski powder". This is certainly not the correct advice and comes from a misunderstanding of what is happening as you ski these conditions. We have already covered how to develop performance on piste and the need to engage the tip of the ski at the top of the turn, the middle of the ski in the apex of the turn and the tail towards the end of the curve. This fore aft pressure control helps you to maximise the design of the modern ski. However, when skiing deeper snow you need to be careful that you do not overload the front of the ski at the top of the turn as this could cause the skis to dive into the snow resulting in an over the handlebars type fall. So, you need to make more use of the middle and tail of the ski but this does NOT mean sitting back. Anyone who does sit back will know that their quadriceps quickly become fatigued because they are using their muscles to hold them up rather than being skeletally aligned.

Therefore you must work the middle and tail of the ski while maintaining a relatively centred position above your feet. You also need to be aware that as your skis move through deep snow they will "plane" at a different angle to the hill which can give a visual impression that the skier is "back" in relation to the slope. The goal should be to allow your tips to come slightly out of the snow towards the end of the turn as can be seen in the photos of Derek & Shona below.

And what about stance, should your feet be close together or apart? In general when skiing deeper snow a slightly closer stance is more effective as it promotes neat skiing and there is less emphasis on edging of your skis. There are many similarities here with skiing bumps. However the best advice is to be adaptable so that if the conditions require you to use greater edge angle then you must adapt your stance accordingly. Remember you ski on two skis and must always have control of both the outer and inner ski of the turn.

Tactically you also need to adapt to the conditions. Your overall speed down the hill will be slower when you are in the snow rather than on top of the snow, so you must adjust your line in order to maintain flow down the mountain. Skiing closer to the fall line is often appropriate with less finish to the turns required.

## Chopped up tracked snow

Skiing chopped up tracked snow, which has not yet been skied enough to make bumps, provides another challenge because the skis can effectively speed up and slow down depending on the depth of snow and how tracked it is! A fun way to approach conditions like this is skiing long radius turns at a good speed. This is where I find you need to be positive and attack the run. You need to be strongly balanced on your outside ski while keeping the inner ski and leg relaxed (but not so relaxed that it fails to copy the outer leg!). Your legs also need to act like shock absorbers to manage the constantly changing surface underneath. It is one of those examples where you need to be strong but relaxed (what almost seems like a contradiction).

You can of course approach the same conditions by skiing shorter radius turns close to the fall line, but unlike bumps where the terrain can be used as a major element in speed control, you need to use effective steering and rounded turn shapes.

*Robbie attacks the chopped up off piste conditions*

### Steeper slopes

We have already looked at one aspect of these variable conditions, the variety of snow conditions that you may encounter, but we must also consider the other variable and that is the changes in terrain & gradient. Again its' fair to say that, when you ski the backcountry, you will encounter constantly changing gradients and terrain that is anything but smooth, (except on those rare virgin powder days). But the greatest challenge that awaits you is coping with steeper slopes.

This is where your technique needs to be solid and your confidence and mind set need to be right (read the section later in this book on training the mind). The steep and deep is very much the domain of the extreme skier, however we are not talking about cliff jumping or big air but merely how to negotiate steep terrain, safely and with good solid technique.

*Derek looks back at the steep slope off the arête on the access to La Vallée Blanche*

Generally speaking you will need a more open stance and hence a low centre of gravity in order to get edge grip on steeper terrain. You can practice a variety of drills to develop your skills in this area such as sideways jumps where you land on the edges without any slip sideways at all. This is also a good way to test the texture and stability of the snow before committing to making linked turns. Also side-slipping where you roll the skis flatter and side slip vertically down the hill and then roll the skis back onto their edges to grip and stop. With practice, you will be able to do this quite quickly so that you have a constant rhythm of releasing and reapplying the edges.

A strong pole plant is essential and will help you to commit to the turn. By planting the pole a little further down the hill and more in line with your toe binding this will open your upper body to the fall line and your direction of travel.

*Siobhain skiing steep terrain, at la Flégère. Notice the open stance and edge grip in the first shot and the solid pole plant with the upper body committed to the direction of travel in the second shot*

Jump turns are really a natural development from edge control and pole plant exercises and are particularly useful on steep and narrow slopes where you want to get the skis around quickly. To do these types of turns efficiently you need to once again focus on turning your legs / feet more than the upper body with the pivot point under your feet. Remember the bracquage (pivoting on the line) exercise from earlier in the book? Jump turns really test all the skiing skills; leg extension / flexion, leg rotation, balance, agility etc. It is better to start practicing these turns on easier terrain and gradually moving onto steeper and steeper slopes.

*The Couloir Poubelle which is accessed from the top of the Bochard on the Grands Montets runs down towards the Mer de Glace which is at the bottom of the Vallée Blanche. Having last skied it in 2006, with Robbie Fenlon, I can say that it is very much "jump turn" terrain!*

## 3.3.2 Off Piste & Backcountry

(by Robbie Fenlon)

Preface layout

The terms off piste skiing, backcountry skiing, and ski touring often get confused. The most current definition I could find is from Wikipedia, an up to date online encyclopaedia

*"**Backcountry skiing** is **skiing** in a sparsely inhabited **rural** region over ungroomed and unmarked slopes or **pistes**. More importantly, the land and the snow pack are not monitored, patrolled, or maintained. Fixed mechanical means of ascent such as **ski lifts** are typically not present."*

*"Off-piste" skiing can refer to any skiing a few metres away from marked trails and slopes, whereas "backcountry" skiing refers to skiing which is not near marked slopes at all, or cannot be accessed by ski-lifts. Backcountry skiing can also involve multi-day trips through snow camping or the use of mountain huts where available."*

In this part of segment 3 I am going to discuss backcountry and off piste skiing. Although their respective definitions differ, these sports involve many similar intellectual and physical skills. In other words, to go backcountry or off piste skiing, you need to know some stuff and you need to be able to do some stuff. The objective of the present segment is to introduce the different skill sets and knowledge in digestible chunks in order to give you the reader a larger picture of the backcountry ski universe.

As an overview of where the skills and knowledge fit, I will describe a typical backcountry skiing day. I will then revisit the various aspects of the day and drill down through each subject to consider each of them in greater depth, from essentials to the more subtle detail.

*Fresh tracks in "Italian" backcountry*

*Photo courtesy of Wilderplaces*

Introduction- Backcountry skiing - the joys and risks

Quite often you hear backcountry skiing described only in terms of its risks and dangers.  It is equally important to emphasize the challenges and satisfaction to be gained by escaping the manufactured environment of the ski station.  When you take this step out of a controlled environment you take on new challenges. You leave behind our man made comforts-no piste maps, no route markers, no groomed tracks, no restaurants. You can still use chair lifts and cable cars but even these can be left behind if you are prepared to be adventurous. The transition between the piste skiing and the backcountry skiing is akin to what you make when moving from a forest park to the jungle or from a swimming pool to the open sea. Once you have taken on the challenge of this raw environment you have to be able to look after yourself.  Thus you need extra knowledge and new skills.

Primarily you need to know where you are. Hence the skill of navigation is very important.  You need to be able to manage your skis and ski technique in what ever type of snow you find. Instead of the mountain being adapted to you, you have to adapt to the mountain. Since you are now skiing in a wild environment there is a risk of being avalanched. Thus you need to be able to minimize the risks. You want to be able to find good snow and slopes to ski on. Weather conditions now become far more threatening as you may be far from shelter if a storm arrives or you are delayed for any reason. Finally, since you may be out of range of ski patrol rescue you need to avoid accidents and be prepared to deal with them yourself if they should arise.

Flow of a typical day

**Starting at home –**
**Research the avalanche risk and identify possible areas of good snow**

Before you leave home you can get a very good idea of the snow conditions both in terms of where the good skiing might be and where the dangers are. Most ski areas have an avalanche bulletin on the internet. At the very least they will give you a weather forecast that will include important information like wind direction, estimated snow fall and freezing level.

A good avalanche report will tell you what the avalanche risk is and which slopes are most at risk, generally in terms of altitude (the height) and aspect (the way the slope faces).

Other information is where to find the best snow for skiing. Generally an avalanche report will tell you the depth of snow that has fallen and the snow conditions at various altitudes. Using your previous experience you can start guessing where the best powder or spring snow might be found.

**Equipment and preparation**

Once you go outside the controlled area (basically anywhere that has not been groomed by a piste basher) you need to be able to look after yourself and your friends. This means being able to navigate, manage any accidents and being properly clothed and equipped for the weather and snow conditions you are likely to encounter. You will need to carry a back pack.

**Your navigation kit** – should be as follows- a local map of 1;50000 scale or 1;25000 and a compass. Extra items that may be useful are an altimeter and GPS

**Your first aid and rescue kit** – a basic first aid kit to deal with minor cuts and sprains. Generally once an injury is anyway complicated most people will need professional assistance to deal with the situation.

**Rescue kit** – an avalanche transceiver – a snow shovel and an avalanche probe. The principal here is that the first 30 minutes after an avalanche are the most important for saving lives. So you and your friends are the first line of rescue. You need the equipment to carry out a rescue yourselves.

**Back pack** – you need this to carry the equipment above. A small neat pack with a waist strap and a chest strap is required and it is important that your pack fits closely to your body and does not move around as you ski energetically.

**Suitable clothing** – without going into to much detail ski clothing for off piste backcountry skiing must be capable of dealing with sometimes severe weather conditions. If the weather turns bad you may not be able to able to shelter in the nearest restaurant.

*A small avalanche*

*Photo courtesy of Wilderplaces*

### First tracks and observations

When you arrive at the ski station you will have access to even more information from a variety of sources. There may be an avalanche bulletin posted on a notice board. There will be a flag indicating the estimated risk for the day. Information will be available from the ski patrol, local skiers or ski shop personnel. Local people generally have a good idea of the risks on a particular day. So before your skis even touch the snow you should have a reasonable idea of snow conditions and risk.

## Check your avalanche transceivers

Even if everyone thinks they have checked already it is important that before the group starts that all transceivers are verified.

## Personal observation and warm up

Once you actually start to ski, do a few warm up runs and look around, try and gauge what is happening to the snow. How much has fallen? Is there any sign of avalanches in the surrounding area and slopes? Did you hear the ski patrol detonating charges in the snow pack earlier?

As you ski keep your eyes and ears open for indications of what is happening. The more you do this the better you become at it.

Important information to look out for is;
• Signs of recent avalanche activity
• Depth and amount of snow fallen
• Wind – Watch to see if there is snow being moved around by wind. This is an important danger sign
• A rise in temperature

All of your observations will make more sense if you have educated yourself with some background knowledge about snow pack stability and weather conditions in mountain areas.

## Safe skiing strategies and group management

Now that you have warmed up with a few runs in controlled areas, you have observed the snow and the surrounding area you may feel confident to try a few off piste runs.

## Questions and judgments

Rather than jumping straight on to that slope you have been waiting to ski all season, it is far more advisable to ski a few easier safer off piste runs first. Choose one based on the following criteria;

• A slope of an easier angle
• A slope that has already been controlled by the ski patrol
• A slope that is reasonably short and has a good run out
• One that is not threatened by an avalanche from above

Before you ski a slope you should ask the following questions;

• If this slope did go (if it avalanched) where would it be likely to fracture?
• If this slope avalanches how big an avalanche could it make?
• If it goes what will I do – where will I escape to?
• Am I sure it won't avalanche?

If you know how to answer these questions and feel confident in your judgment then you are ready to ski the slope.

Even when you have decided that a slope is safe to ski it does not mean you throw caution to the wind. There are strategies you can use to make your skiing safer. They are based on the principle that the worst thing you can do is adopt a free for all / every man for himself approach.

The best strategies allow for good team work and observation;

• Choose a safe area to start from and a safe area to stop
• Break the slope up in to several shorter runs
• Ski one at a time this way if anyone is avalanched they will be observed by the others and will have rescue available. It also means that less weight is put on the snow pack

- Make sure the stopping area is really safe just in case an avalanche should be triggered above you by a following skier

## Choosing a safe line

On any given slope there may be some lines that are safer than others. The line is the route you choose to get from A to B. Here are a few simple tips;

- Avoid any convexity in the slope if possible
- Stay visible to the rest of you group. If you ski out of sight and something happens they may not react until too late
- Stay away from cliff edges (unless you really know what you are doing). If a slope goes and you get carried over it might hurt!
- Start from somewhere safe and ski to somewhere safe
- Make sure you can see a long distance ahead of you. You are moving fast and if an obstacle suddenly has to be avoided (a rock, a crevasse, a hidden hole) you need to have time see it and then to react

## Snow types

One use of snow knowledge is to avoid getting avalanched but another very useful by product is knowing how and where to find the best snow for skiing. In general snow falls into the following classifications; powder, spring snow, crusty snow (either wind crust, sun crust or rain crust), hard pack and crud (which describes everything else).

- Powder- untracked powder is what we all long to find. The deeper the better (well so we think). Powder comes in different weights and textures from light, loose and cold to slightly moist and heavier. The depth of the snow and the steepness of the slope make a difference as to how enjoyable it is to ski

- Spring snow is also very enjoyable to ski. You find it where the snow pack has melted and refrozen many times. Then when the hard surface has melted and softened it gives a really wonderful skiing surface. Nature's piste!
- Crust- This is hard to ski especially if it supports you some of the time and then breaks unexpectedly. A breakable crust is like skiing over rat traps. The crust can be formed by melting and refreezing by either sun or rain. Or it can be formed by a wind deposited layer
- Hard pack is snow that has been packed down either by a lot of skiers or wind action. It has a chalky surface and if it supports your weight it can be great fun to ski
- Crud- Everything else – but generally it is snow that has already been chopped up by other skiers

**How to find the good snow**
Read the avalanche and snow report.

- Find out where the freezing level is as you won't get good powder below the freezing level
- Stay away from wind affected snow straight after snow fall as this is a high avalanche risk
- Find snow that has fallen loose and not been affected by the wind
- Generally look for slopes out of direct sunlight. Shaded  areas tend to keep the powder cooler and better to ski (but beware if there is an avalanche risk as it stays longer in the shaded areas)
- Higher up tends to be deeper if there has not been strong winds

- If the visibility is bad high up and it is still snowing ski in a forested area. It is easier to see and there is generally less risk of avalanche
- If you are patient and privileged enough to live in a ski area where the snow does not get skied immediately after it has fallen leave the snow some time to settle before you ski it (one or two days). Wait for a clear day. That way you get safer snow conditions and clear visibility for skiing (many people ignore this precaution in busy ski areas and accidents and fatalities are the result)

For spring snow you need to get your timing right if you ski too early the surface is still hard, too late and the skis sink too deep into the snow.

### Get home safely

Navigation – you should be keeping track of where you are throughout the day. Sometimes it is tempting to relax towards the end of the day. This can lead to a bad navigation decision and extra hours wasted getting home.

The last part of the day is a time when accidents can happen due to either tiredness or relaxed vigilance. Keep paying attention to the snow conditions until you are safely back in the car park.

## Some useful basic principles

**The three basic rules – wind – precipitation – temperature change.**

One of the things I have noticed in my time as a mountain guide is that people associate avalanche awareness and mountain safety skills mainly with digging holes in the snow and charging around the place with electronic beepers looking for other buried beepers.

In my opinion the main reason people get taught these skills is that they are easy skills to teach and students have the impression that they have learnt something because they can dig a hole in the snow and identify layers in the snow pack.

The truth is that what you have learnt is that there are layers in the snow pack and that snow shovels are good for digging holes.

The much more important knowledge is gained from observing the snow conditions under your feet and in the bigger environment around you. Also be aware of the weather history over recent days and weeks as this contributes to your overall knowledge of the snow pack. The observations you make should be backed up by theoretical knowledge provided from books, weather forecasts and websites. Then as a useful educational activity by all means dig holes in the snow. It is the only way you are going to learn that the snow pack is a complicated layered material.

**There are three basic principles that are fundamental to causing avalanches and although they are common knowledge they are often ignored.**

Some days without even going outside the door I have known ordinary cafe owners in Chamonix to have a better idea of the avalanche risk than experienced ski bums.

**The three basic rules (break them at your own risk)**

**Avalanche risk increases if:**
1.  **It snows or rains or there is any precipitation. The greater the precipitation generally the greater the risk**
2.  **If it is windy and snowing. OR even if it is just windy and no snow has fallen in a few days**
3.  **The temperature rises**

With no greater knowledge than this you can increase your safety margin many times if you take the necessary precautions.

I am speaking from direct experience of getting away with ignoring these conditions from time to time then paying the price for my over confidence.

Every time we experience these conditions during winter and spring in the Alps we get avalanches to a greater or lesser extent. If the conditions have been fairly active, we are guaranteed to read an article in the local newspaper about a death or injury due to an avalanche.

*Photo courtesy of Wilderplaces*

## Snow stuff

**Why slopes avalanche and how to avoid being there when it happens**

On the rare occasions that it snows in Ireland we only get one layer of snow stuck to the ground. In the parts of the world where we go to ski there are multiple layers laid down over a period of months. Every new snow fall creates a new layer. The combination of all these layers is referred to as the **snow pack**.

The snow pack has a life cycle of its own. There are many environmental factors that change and transform it; air temperature, ground temperature, different temperatures within the snow pack, the effects of rain, wind and sun. And the weight of the snow pack. In many ways it is like a big layer cake that is being cooked at various temperatures then transferred to a fridge and refrozen. Obviously all this cooking and freezing process added to all the other variables is going to affect the snow CAKE!

In addition to all the above, at a microscopic level there are changes in the snow flakes that effect how they bond to each other.

Change is not necessarily a bad thing. But the main thing you need to know is that the layers in the snow pack do not stick to each other all that well at times.

Imagine our layer cake. A layer of sponge cake, a big thick layer of cream, then a big slab of fruit cake on top. Imagine the slabs of cake are several metres squared in size. The cake is sitting on a table. No problem so far. But lift one end of the cake so it is now at a 30 degree angle to the horizontal and what happens.

Splodge! Cake slides all over the floor

This negative aspect of the snow pack is a quality of which you need to be hyper aware.

The basic principle is that layers in the snow pack can slide over each other. Some times these layers can be metres thick. Another factor we tend to forget is that snow doesn't just stick to the snow below it but to the snow all around it. This means that a layer of snow the size of a football pitch (or bigger at times) can be released in an avalanche.

This is what makes avalanches really dangerous. When they release they often slide in large slab like pieces. It seems that the whole mountain side is moving.

## Types of Avalanche

**The most dangerous avalanche type for skiers is the slab avalanche.**

This is the avalanche type that catches skiers in 90 percent of cases. The statistics are very revealing; 75% or more of avalanche victims are caught by slab avalanches. **95% of avalanches are triggered by the people who are caught in them.**

Being caught in a slab avalanche is similar to walking on a frozen lake. Suddenly there is a crack and everything around you starts to move.

The slab itself is an area of snow that has bonded together across its surface. It may be as large as a football field or the size of a mattress. Although the surface may be strong enough to support a person's weight, it may be resting on a weak layer buried in the snow. This can rupture and allow the slab to slide down the mountain......with you on it - then in it.

**Slabs** are generally formed by wind deposited snow, either during a snowfall or, in the period after recent snowfall. The wind carries the snow and deposits it in areas sheltered from the wind (the leeward side of the slope).

Wind slab danger areas are generally close to a ridge line or any other area where the wind slows down and deposits its load of snow.

A simple rule of thumb is that if the wind is blowing from the west it will deposit snow on the eastern side of the mountain near crests and ridges. Avoid those areas!

### Wet snow avalanches

These avalanches are simpler to understand and easier to predict. Basically when the snow warms up it becomes sludgy and then slides down the hill. The big clue for this type of avalanche is a sharp rise in temperature. The risk is even higher if there is a sharp rise in temperature after a recent snow fall.

### Funny crystals and the refrigerated danger layer

Transformations that take place within the snow pack are hidden from the observer. Snow crystals transform naturally. How they transform is affected by temperatures in the snow pack.

One really dangerous crystal that can form in the snow pack is a beast called the faceted crystal. This forms during periods of very stable calm weather, on the shaded or cooler slopes of the mountain. One of the reasons it is so dangerous is that people become less cautious of avalanche risk when the weather is good and stable for an extended period.

The working principle is that the ground is relatively warm under the snow and the air is cold above the snow. Hence vapour migrates upwards through the snow pack creating a weak layer of sugar like crystals at the base of the snow pack. The whole weight of the snow pack becomes supported by this sugary base layer. It is very unstable. When these crystals exist in the snow pack many large avalanches can be expected to occur.

There are many other types of crystal formations that exist but they would take a whole book to explain.

**To summarize this section**; The snow pack is made of many layers. Some of these layers are weak and if they fracture an avalanche can occur. Weak layers are caused by different factors, some by external factors such as wind sun and rain others by internal changes in the snow pack.

Most avalanche victims have triggered the avalanche that killed them. The most common type of avalanche to catch skiers is the wind slab avalanche.

## Avalanche Terrain

### Slope angle
If you read the statistics for avalanche accidents you will find that the majority of them occur on slopes of 35 to 45 degrees. The slope angle with the highest occurrence of avalanches is 38 degrees.

### Convexity
Snow is spread on the mountain side in a big blanket. This blanket has a certain tensile strength. It tends to tear on parts of the slope that put it under tension. Tension occurs where the slope is convex.

### Ridges and crests
Wind slab avalanches tend to occur near ridges on the hill side or near a crest or summit. This is because the wind tends to deposit snow as a hard or soft slab on the sheltered side of these features.

### Gullies and couloirs

Although they can be very interesting and exciting places to ski they also act as a natural funnel for any avalanche debris. So do not stop and stand in the middle of a gully. Move out of it or at least move to a sheltered area at the side.

### Cornices

These are dangerous over hangs of snow found on the crests and summits of mountains. It is dangerous to stand on them or near them as they collapse. It is also dangerous to traverse under them for the same reason. They are especially unstable in warm weather.

### Cliffs

Although it has become fashionable to jump off cliffs on skis most mere mortals should avoid skiing near cliffs. If you ski above them even a small avalanche may carry you over the edge. If you ski near an edge and slip a minor slip can become a major fall. Many skiers (some very well know extreme skiers) have been killed in falls from cliffs in recent years.

### Terrain traps

Think of an ordinary house hold bath. How much snow does it take to fill a bath? That's how much snow it takes to bury you! If you are on an open flat slope a small avalanche may run around your ankles. The same avalanche coming down into a confined gully may bury you.

Pay attention to the shape of the terrain around you. In the wrong area even a minor avalanche can have serious consequences.

## Skiing stuff

**Safe ski strategies revisited**

Although I mentioned safe skiing strategies earlier I would like to revisit them in more detail. Employing a safe ski strategy is probably one the most useful things you can do to reduce your exposure to avalanche risk. Simply by managing yourself and your group you increase your safety margin.

**Organising the group**

The principles we apply to managing a group on piste apply to off piste skiing as well. If everyone is skiing at once with no defined leader or destination chaos usually results. Simple things you can do to organise the group are as follows;

- Decide on a lead skier and a back marker
- Start skiing from a defined area to a defined area
- Keep lines of communication open and make sure everybody is aware of the overall plan

**Skiing one at a time**

- Ski the slope one at a time – this puts less load on the snow pack (and less weight on any weak layer)
- All members of the group watch the person skiing
- If there is an avalanche have a rescue plan (that you have already practiced)
- Only when you know a slope is really safe to ski should you consider skiing as an organised group

*Photo courtesy of Wilderplaces*

### Watching out for each other

- When skiing off the piste people can fall in deep snow (it can be difficult to get up) so make sure that a strong skier is at the back to help anyone who needs help
- If everyone skis without paying attention to others there can be collisions (powder euphoria is distracting!)
- If someone falls and loses a ski (especially at the back of the group) make sure you have not gone so far that you cannot return to help

## Choosing areas of safety

When a group stops off piste it is important to choose a safe area away from avalanche risk. Look for places as below;

- Out of the line of any possible avalanche from above
- Away from cornices and the middle of gullies
- On a flatter area where it is easy to stand (not bunched together in the middle of a steep gully)
- Beneath the protection of a rock out crop
- If none of the above exists try and imagine the trajectory of any possible avalanche and stay clear of it

## Choosing a safe line

One girl's safe line is another girl's extreme ski descent. How safe a line is will depend on your ski ability. But in the case of avalanche risk there are certain areas to avoid;

- Cornices and just beneath cornices is where you find unstable wind pack snow (wind slabs)
- Convexities – in avalanche terrain a convexity on the slope is like a dotted line saying tear here
- Try and link areas of safety
- Ski on a ridge line rather than in a gully, especially if there is a risk of wind slab
- Choose a line where the group can see each other at all times

## Breaking up the journey

We sometimes have the tendency to just go for it and ski the whole slope in one go. It is good to stop and regroup every now and then as;

- It allows time to re-examine the line of descent and change if need be

• It allows everyone time to regain their breath and refocus

**Finally**
Always be prepared to turn around and go back!

Employing the above strategies may slow you down at first but it increases your safety margin immensely and as you gain practice you can ski efficiently and safely.

## Snow pits

**Quite often students leave an avalanche awareness class thinking that it is all about digging holes in the snow. Snow pits are only one small part of a much greater body of knowledge needed to travel safely in backcountry terrain.**

*Photo courtesy of Wilderplaces*

Snow pits are easy to dig, but they are hard to understand. It takes a lot of experience and knowledge to make sense of them. Realistically most guides and ski instructors do not dig snow pits while they are skiing off piste. They use all the other information that I have mentioned earlier to help them create a picture of what is happening in the snow pack.

What you will see guides, instructors and other ski professionals doing is a lot of poking and probing in the snow. Then they examine closer by digging a quick pit with their hand or a ski pole. This way they get a feel for what is going on in the snow pack but with a more global perspective.

These quick tests are adding information to the picture they have already constructed from all the previous observations they have made up to that point.

The reason a snow pit is useful to a snow pack novice is that it can introduce some basic concepts. Digging a hole in the snow can teach people the following concepts;

- Layers exist in the snow pack
- Some layers are of different consistency to others
- There are a few different quick tests you can use to recognise different layers
- There are a few simple tests that can show weak bonding between layers in the snow pack
- There are different crystal types in the snow pack (but you really need to know what you are looking at to make sense of them)

Snow pits are just one piece of the jigsaw of information that allows us to determine what is happening in the snow pack.

I think at an early stage in your avalanche interpretation skills it is better to trust avalanche reports and observations rather than make sketchy guesses based on holes you dig in the snow.

Use snow pits as a learning tool. Dig them to understand the archaeology of snow fall. Familiarise yourself with the idea that there is a lot of physics happening under your feet as you ski off the piste.

## Transceiver stuff

**Rescuing buried friends**

**Transceivers do not protect you from avalanches.**

**The reason you wear one is so that other people can find you when you have messed up with all the other stuff we have been discussing.**

**Learning how to use a transceiver is easy compared to learning how to avoid getting avalanched. Yet many people wear them and do not know how to use them. Worse still they learned how to once and think they will remember how to use them during a stressful accident situation - This is wishful thinking.**

**Finally and most importantly if someone is buried under snow, time is of the essence. The quicker you find the victim the higher their chance of survival. The first 30 minutes after burial are crucial. When you consider this factor one thing becomes clear – waiting for a rescue team is a waste of time. YOU ARE THE RESCUE TEAM. So get practicing.**

*Photo courtesy of Wilderplaces*

## Transceivers the basics – how they work

Avalanche transceivers are basically radio transmitters and receivers. Each unit has two basic modes – send and receive. Any transceiver in receive mode can detect any other transceiver in transmit mode. They generally have a range of between 20 and 50 metres.

## Using a transceiver

- All transceivers are worn in transmit mode
- When you put your transceiver on you make sure it is turned on
- One member of the party should always do a function check on all the other transceivers in the party
- Make sure your transceiver is on at all times. Do not take it off or turn it off until you are safely back in the valley
- Even if you do not know how to use a transceiver to find another you have a much greater chance of being rescued after and avalanche accident if you are wearing one

## Using one transceiver to find another

Rather than covering all the user instructions of all the transceivers on the market I will focus on a few basic exercises you can use to practice using your transceiver.

At the risk of stating the obvious here are a few recommendations as to how you can teach yourself to use a transceiver;

## Stage 1

1. Read the owner's manual
2. Learn how to turn the unit on and off and how to set it to send and receive

## Stage 2

Once you have these basics get another transceiver unit and turn it to transmit. Put your unit on to receive and look at the read out on the unit. Move away from the transmitter and watch for changes on the display screen. Listen for changes in the tone. Get used to the different tones and displays associated with your unit.

## Stage 3

Working with a partner on a flat snow covered area (but you can use any area that you can camouflage the location of the unit). One person buries a transmitting transceiver under a shallow layer of snow- the other person then tries to use their transceiver to locate the unit. You both practice this until you become very efficient. Increase the depth of the burial and the distance of the search (but remain within the receiving range). When you feel you have mastered this move on to the next exercise.

## Stage 4

Working with a partner: Simulate a more realistic rescue scenario. Put the transceiver in a rucksack to create a larger object to find;

1. At first bury the sack nearby and use your avalanche probe to find at a known burial location. Get used to the sensation of locating an object with the probe
2. One person buries the sack and a (transmitting) transceiver within a 50 metre radius of the searcher. The searcher must now find the buried transceiver using their own transceiver an avalanche probe and shovel
3. As you get better at this bury the object deeper and further away until eventually you can locate the object quickly

## Stage 5

Now you are ready to simulate a real avalanche incident.

One person buries the sack and transceiver in a chosen avalanche zone (out of sight from the searcher).

The buried transceiver should be beyond the range of the searching transceiver.

There are a few important concepts to introduce at this point. When somebody gets buried by avalanche debris their transceiver may be out of range of any rescuers transceiver. Thus there are different phases of the search process;

1. The primary search phase – where you are looking for the first evidence of a transceiver signal
2. The secondary search phase – where you have located the signal and you are homing in quickly to the area of the burial
3. The pinpoint (or final search) phase – where you know you are close to the victim and you use a precise location method to exactly locate the signal before probing and digging

The searcher now starts the exercise first trying to find the signal and then homing in on it as quickly as possible. Then pinpoint, search, probe, dig and recover the "victim".

Both partners should keep practicing this exercise until they can locate a transceiver in less than 5 minutes.

**Stage 6**

Multiple burials; to start with you can practice this finding two transceivers buried within range. When you have mastered this move on to burying two rucksacks, with transceivers, and search as in stage 5. If you get good at this bury more victims.

**Stage 7**

This is when the exercise simulates as closely as possible a real life avalanche scenario.

Imagine a group of 6 people have been out skiing off piste. Two people have already skied down and are waiting in a safe area. A third person starts to ski and triggers a large slab avalanche which buries them. Unfortunately the 2 people below did not choose a safe enough area to wait and they too are buried.

Now 3 people are buried and there are 3 rescuers. If you imagine that you have three friends buried under the snow, in the process of suffocating, it is understandable that stress and fear levels in the rescue group are going to be quite high, hence not conducive to clear and confident decision making. This is where having a practised routine is really going to make a difference.

Managing the group dynamic is very important. Who is going to do what? Is everybody going to search? Or is there perhaps a better way of organising the group. The answers to these questions will depend on the experience of the rescuers and how much they have practiced.

I suggest that in a situation like this it is good to designate one person to stay at the start of the search area and keep an overview of the situation (a site manager). Then the two others can search different areas of the avalanche zone. The person who remains above has an overall idea of how the searching is going and can be calling the rescue services for back up. Meanwhile the searchers can focus on what they are doing knowing that there is someone keeping an eye on the over all situation. If a transceiver is pinpointed the site manager can move in to assist in digging the victim out.

As you practice at this level you can design different scenarios and designate different tasks to different people. Some roles that might be useful are;

- Dedicated diggers (people with shovels)
- Site managers (people with an overview and command of the situation)
- Dedicated searchers (people with transceivers)
- Stand by and back up diggers
- First aid person

There are books, websites and videos dedicated to these subjects and it is beyond the scope of this segment to go into these details.

Use the exercises I have described above along with the user manual for your transceiver and you can teach yourself the basics. The most important thing is to actually practice because a real situation is very stressful and anything that is learnt from a book will be confusing and slow to apply to a real life situation.

## Ski touring and skinning

*A busy day in the Norwegian backcountry*

*Photo courtesy of Wilderplaces*

Skiers generally think of their skis as only to be used for going downhill. The idea of walking uphill – especially in ski boots is often regarded as evidence of insanity.

I came into skiing from the sport of mountaineering so walking up hills was not an alien concept. Therefore my perception of skis was that they were to be used for travelling in the mountains in much the same way that a bike can be used to cover more distance on a road than by walking. Skis are the most efficient way to travel in the mountains.

Question: why would a skier be interested in walking up a hill?

Answer 1; because not many people do, so that's how you get to the untracked powder snow!

Answer 2; because there is not always a chair lift built to get you to the slope you want to ski.

Answer 3; walking opens up the whole mountain to you and you can travel through the mountains on your skis if you are prepared to make the effort. Travelling through the mountains on skis is referred to as ski touring or backcountry skiing.

**Becoming a backcountry skier**

There are two ways to walk as a skier. One is to put your skis on your back pack and walk in your boots. This is commonly referred to as boot packing. The other is to get a pair of touring bindings fitted to your skis and stick skins to the base. This allows you to walk uphill on your skis. This is called skinning.

Skinning and ski touring are not hard to do. Any skier can walk on skins. Basically if you can walk you can skin. The only movement that people find awkward is the kick turn which is used when zig zagging up a slope.

*An uphill kick turn*

*Photo courtesy of Wilderplaces*

There are other skills to be learnt when becoming a good ski tourer or backcountry skier. But in general the basic skills that we have discussed earlier in this segment are all relevant to ski touring.

To remind you I will re iterate them;

- Mountain navigation
- Avalanche awareness skills
- Avalanche accident rescue skills
- Mountain Weather knowledge
- Reasonable off piste skiing skills
- Safe skiing skills

As you progress with your ski touring and become more adventurous you will add other skill sets such as;

- Mountaineering skills
- Glacier travel skills
- Rope work skills
- Snow and ice climbing skills

Even with basic skiing skills and reasonable fitness you can begin ski touring.

Off piste skiing and backcountry skiing (ski touring) expand your horizons way beyond the piste. If you consider how much of the world's mountains are covered in snow and how few of those mountain areas have ski lifts one begins to realise that backcountry skiing opportunities are vast.

## Navigation for skiers

*Photo courtesy of Wilderplaces*

## Why bother learning to navigate

Once you move off the piste you are moving on to the unmanaged and unmarked mountain. The piste map does not work any more. You are going to need a real map.

Maps suitable for skiers' navigation will be either 1:50000 scale or 1;25000 scale.

Here are some reasons you might want to learn to use a map.

## The pain and danger of getting lost

Most accidents in the mountains start with people being lost. They then become tired and stressed then make mistakes. This can be especially stressful if the weather is bad or you are with inexperienced skiers or children.

Knowing where you are at all times and knowing where you are going are very important factors in safe skiing.

## The resulting accidents

Being lost leads to accidents. A classic off piste accident scenario starts with people getting lost. They then continue downhill hoping to find a track but find themselves lost in forest or above a cliff. Some people manage to extract themselves from this situation with a lot of effort and stress. Others are not so lucky. Most years we read in the newspapers of an accident where some skier has skied over a cliff accidentally. They were lost!

## Being late

If you do not know where you are or where you are going then you have little chance of knowing how long your journey is going to take. This can lead to all sorts of complications including being caught out in the dark or missing last chair lifts.

## Navigation for Skiers

Navigation is a practical skill best learned in the outdoors. Hence my approach in this part of the segment is to identify skills that you might practice yourself.

Rather than going into detailed explanations I will give you the outline of the task you need to be able to manage. It is then up to you to get a map and go outside and practice.

Below I identify the main navigation skills needed by skiers;

## Where am I on the mountain?

This is probably one for the most useful skills you can learn. Once you can do this, you can plan where to go from there.

## Where do I find the best slopes to ski (for my level of ability)?

If you can read a map properly you should be able to determine how steep a slope is, what direction it faces and how to get to it (and get off it).

## Which slopes do I think are at risk of avalanche and how do I avoid them?

Armed with all your avalanche awareness knowledge you should be able to look at a map and work out where the best snow to ski might be found. More importantly you should be able to determine which slopes to avoid due to avalanche risk;

## 1. Identify the slope first by aspect and then altitude

When reading an avalanche bulletin you will always find information telling you which aspect of slope is predicted to be most exposed to avalanche risk. Often a report will say there is a danger of wind slab avalanches on north and east facing slopes above 2000 metres.

### 2. Find ways to avoid them

Armed with the above information you should be able to look at your map and choose slopes that are not exposed to this avalanche risk.

### How do I learn to navigate?

You can start learning to navigate from your own home. All you need is a map. Buy one for an area you already know and try to see how places you are familiar with are marked on the map.

### Start at home

Learn to relate a map to the landscape then the landscape to the map.

The essence of reading a map is to be able to see the map as a picture of a landscape. When you look at the map you should be able to imagine what the depicted landscape might look like.

The next stage is to take the map into the actual landscape (the same landscape as is depicted on the map). Now try to look at features in the landscape and see how and where they are marked on the map. This skill is called feature recognition and it is the basis of navigation.

### Learn to set a map

Setting a map means lining up the map with features on the ground. If a road runs north to south hold the map so that the same road on the map is running north to south. Another way to do this is to find out where north is using a compass and face the top of the map north (maps are always drawn with the north to the top of the map).

Once you have this skill refined you will be able to tell which direction you have to travel to get to your chosen point on the map.

**Learn to read contour lines**
What height are you at and which way is the slope facing?

The next skill is being able to interpret contour lines. These are lines that join points of equal height on the map. Being able to read contour detail will allow you to extract important skiing information from the map;

- How steep is the slope (how close together are the contour lines)?
- What direction does it face (slope aspect – the way the slope faces is perpendicular to the contour lines- slope aspect is the same direction as the fall line)? This is important for determining the ski conditions and avalanche conditions of a slope
- What altitude are you starting and finishing at? How long is your run going to be? Is the snow going to be cool powder or warm heavy sludge?

**Navigation can be learned at home in Ireland**
You do not need to be in the Alps or the Rockies to learn to navigate. You can practice in the Irish hills. Hill walking is good for your ski fitness as well as your navigation skills. Get a map and compass and go for a walk in Wicklow or better still the west of Ireland or Kerry.

**Applying that to your skiing (get a map of your ski area)**
To take your home learned navigation skills to the next level buy a real map next time you go on a ski holiday. Instead of using, (or as well as), the piste map use a real map to find your way around the ski area and;

- Try and identify the hills and mountains around you
- Try to identify the ski lifts on the map
- As you become more skilled try and identify the slope aspect you are skiing on
- Read the map to determine what altitude you are at
- Follow the line of your journey as you ski around the resort

**The skills you are expected to have as a competent navigator**
- Self location (where am I?)
- Feature recognition (being able to recognise the mountains and landscape features around you)
- Recognise slope aspect
- Be able to determine your altitude
- Be able to follow your journey on a map
- Be able to recognise potential risks and dangers on the map. Cliffs – potential avalanche slopes – ridge lines that may have cornices or wind slab accumulations
- Be able to recognise slopes that may have really good ski conditions

**Using a compass**
You can navigate without a compass. Quite often people confuse themselves with compasses. Learn to read a map first.

At a basic level of navigation there are only three skills you need to master with a compass;
- Be able to find north with a compass
- Be able to set a map with a compass
- Be able to take a bearing with a compass

Other compass skills are beyond the scope of this book.

# Record of Notes, Thoughts & Ideas

*Liam Williams skiing at les Grands Montets, Argentière*

*Photo by Alasdair Scobbie*

# Segment 4 – Fit 4 Skiing

## 4.1    Cross Training
(by Liam Williams)

Skiing as a sporting or leisure activity is very exhilarating. It can be enjoyed by people of all ages from 3 year old children sliding down gentle slopes right through to 80 year olds just looking  to have a good day out, and all the racers and free skiers in between. Skiing should be fun, safe and enjoyable. Because skiing is both mentally and physically challenging, to get the most out of your ski experience on snow, it is a good idea to be both physically and mentally prepared. The first part of this segment looks at "cross training" which essentially covers other sports and fitness training that is useful for skiing. The second part then looks at how you can prepare yourself mentally giving ideas on some practical tools that you can use.

How much preparation you put into it depends on several factors. For example your age might be one factor. It might be enough for a young child to wrap up warm at the weekends and enjoy a few hours out in the garden, instead of being stuck to the television or using the latest computer games, or for some it might be of benefit to get into the habit of walking more often, even if it is only up to the shop for the paper.

Most of us who have ever gone on a ski holiday regret the very first day not having done more, before our trip, to be physically more prepared. Even the act of getting yourself and all the necessary equipment to the bottom of the lift station can leave some feeling the worse for wear. Like anything else the more you put into the preparation for your ski trip the more you will get out of it. If you are not living within easy access to a snow covered ski resort you will have to do all your preparation and training on dry land. But, do not despair, there is a lot you can do on dry land to ensure an exhilarating and fun filled time on the snow.

If you are fortunate enough to live near an artificial slope or snow-dome you can use it to improve your ski technique. This saves you wasting the beginning of your holiday reacclimatising to the feel of your skis and helps bring you back to the level you were at on your previous trip.

In terms of physical preparation, for those of you who are more adventurous and who hope to meet all the challenges that the mountain throws at you, be that a need for speed, or the thrill of fresh powder snow, or the challenge and unpredictability of bumps and variable terrain, nearly all sports can help you to some degree, but some more so than others.

**Cycling** is an obvious sport to start with. It is accessible to everybody. The muscles predominantly used in cycling are similar to those required in skiing. Firstly let me touch on **mountain biking**. All you need is a mountain bike and access to mountain tracks. The more miles you can put in on the bike the greater the benefit in terms of building up your fitness and endurance. For increasing your strength and power it is important to spend time climbing the hills. Time spent on the variable terrain, prevalent on mountain tracks, is also instrumental in developing your agility and balance. This is a very important skill to develop to prepare you for the variable terrain of the ski slopes.

*Robin Seymour, 2 times Irish Olympian in Cross Country Mountain Biking, 14 times Irish National Mountain Bike Cross Country Champion and 15 times Irish National Cyclo-cross Champion*

*"Photo courtesy of Outsider Magazine"*

**Down-hill mountain biking** is one of the closest experiences you will get for practicing picking your route down the mountain. Like skiing, you have to pick the safest route or the more challenging. You also have to avoid obstacles like trees and adapt your position to meet the constantly changing surface. In addition it helps you become accustomed to travelling downhill at speed and conquer some of the fears that are associated with all adventure sports.

Moving on to **road cycling** which can be enjoyed by those not living close to mountain tracks. The same benefits apply. Hill climbing is good for strength and power and hours spent getting in mileage on the roads builds up endurance. Anything that develops your strength and endurance will prove beneficial when you take to the ski slopes. Cycling in groups is similar to skiing in a group. You need good concentration and to be constantly aware of the people, both in front and around you, while keeping a watchful eye on the terrain.

Lastly on the cycling theme for those cold or wet winter months, if you have access to your local gym you can participate in **spinning classes**. This involves an instructor bringing a group of participants on special "spinning bikes" through a series of resistance changes to mimic that of an uphill, downhill or flat cycle track. The muscle groups predominately used are the same as those used in downhill and cross country skiing. The quadriceps, hamstrings, glutes and calf muscles are all trained. The muscles in the inner and outer thigh can also be trained by incorporating side to side pedal strokes under a higher resistance. Spinning classes also benefit from having the instructor in front of you to motivate you and ensure you get the most benefit from the time and effort put into your training.

**Running** is another sport that can be enjoyed by almost anyone and the benefit shows when you spend long hours on some snow covered mountain. Running as a physical activity can be enjoyed by anyone anywhere. It doesn't involve the purchase of any expensive equipment, merely a decent pair of trainers, nor does it require a specific geographical location. So get out, start running and feel the benefit! **Road running** will benefit your overall fitness and endurance. Similar to the cycling, long steady runs build up your endurance, while shorter hill sprints build up vital strength in your legs. All this will add to your physical preparation for your ski trip, allowing you to concentrate on the ski experience either improving your technique and skills or just enjoying the mountain experience. Remember it is important for skiers of all levels to prepare themselves physically not just for expert skiers. If you want to add variety to your running try **cross country running**. The physical benefits are the same as road running but in addition you learn to adjust to variable terrain, improving both balance and agility, both of which are critical for skiing. Like the mountain biking you need to be constantly alert and aware of your surroundings to be sure and choose a good route. This is a good skill to develop for your skiing. However if you can't run, you should go walking. All physical activity will help.

**Rollerblades**, (also known as inline skates because the four wheels are in a row instead of at the corners like traditional roller skates), are a great tool for not only learning modern ski technique but also maintaining and improving it.

Good protective equipment is essential before trying this sport (helmet, knee, elbow and hand / wrist guards). Rollerblading is a good workout on its own and can be very effective to cross train as pre-season preparation. Suitable areas to practice are bike paths, big promenade areas, industrial areas which are quiet at weekends or anywhere with a smooth surface that is safe and quiet.

While rollerblading mimics the same movements of skiing, you need to be careful not to develop skating-specific movements that may hurt your skiing. Novice skaters tend to A-frame in too wide a stance, bracing from big toe to big toe, which doesn't transfer too effectively to high end skiing. The tendency also is to show excessive shuffle or inside foot lead.

Useful tips

Initiate each turn by tipping the old outside foot over to its little toe side, and keep it tipping in that direction to control turn shape. Graduating from A-frame to matched big / little toe wheel angles is the big break-thru for effective cross training.

Focus on keeping your stance narrow enough to match wheel angles of both feet and turning is very much like skiing. You don't need much pitch, just enough to maintain a constant momentum.

For slalom training, keep the upper body facing down the fall line with more turning of the legs.

For GS the body should be square and more in the direction of travel.

One exercise to help avoid the tendency of guiding with the inside skate and too many skating movements, is to slalom down a paved slope using only one foot. This will improve your ski related muscles and your balance.

Rollerblading is great for the lower body and is fun and convenient. To find out more ask in your local sports shop or search online for any organized meetings in your area. Enjoy yourself and remember to wear protective equipment.

Another way to physically prepare for skiing is to join the **local gym**. Sometimes during the winter months this can be the easiest way to train. With long dark nights it can be difficult to incorporate outdoor training in your daily routine. Most good gyms will have qualified instructors who will prepare programs for you specific to skiing and your general level of fitness. This will include aerobic training for general fitness, on any of the many options now available in gyms, (bicycle, stepper, cross trainer, stair climber, ergo-meter, trotter). There's an option for everyone. It can also include a weights program designed to develop strength and power and various floor exercises to develop agility and fitness.

Progressing on from the gym theme, you can also work with alternative gym equipment, such as gym ball or **Swiss ball**, to develop your balance and agility. You can start by simply sitting on the Swiss ball and trying to balance, then progressing to kneeling or standing on the ball. Various exercises can be added including weights to develop strength and agility. Again the local gym should be able to provide a specific program to meet your needs and capabilities. As an alternative to the Swiss ball try the **BOSU balance trainer**. This is basically a Swiss ball cut in half. A lot can be achieved in your local gym.

Another, less well known, but increasingly popular training tool is a **Vew-do balance board**. A traditional balance board is a deck made from hard wood which sits on top of a cylinder (rock) whereby an individual stands and attempts to balance on the apparatus while spanning the rock in various directions and geometrical planes.

Improving fitness can be tedious but vew-do balance boarding is fun and produces amazing results. Inner balance takes over and adds a feeling of overall well- being. Using a Vew-do board will significantly improve your balance. Standing on it while doing squats, push-ups, or other exercises, provides a real challenge. Improving core strength means strong abs, better posture and long, lean muscles. Vew-do allows you to incorporate balance with effective torso strength training for a dynamic work out. It is also great fun, allowing you to do tricks such as ollies, kickflips, transfers and shove-its, all of which can then be tried out in the fun park up the mountain.

*Vew-do equipment includes a "rock", a "balance board" and a mat. There are a variety of rocks and boards available depending on skill level*

*Vew-do balancing in action! Initially you can allow the board move a lot from side to side then, try to remain as stationary as possible*

There are also sports that one wouldn't necessarily link to ski preparation. **Martial Arts**, is another indoor activity that can be very beneficial for your skiing. For instance in most combative arts you are taught to hold a wide stance with flexed knees, which you start with and return to while throwing different strikes. This rapidly improves overall balance, which is important in skiing.

In skiing, you are also first taught a basic stance that is always returned to (home base), while you negotiate changing terrain and snow conditions such as bumps, steeps, powder, light snow, heavy snow etc. As just described, the same applies to martial arts with progression being indicated by the ease with which the student is able to return to the basic stance after carrying out an attack or defence move. Martial arts training will also help improve your spatial awareness and reduce the number of times you find yourself out of balance. Simply trying a straightforward front kick over and over again will help with controlling your balance which in turn will help when you are skiing over changing terrain because you learn to cancel out unnecessary movements.

And if you are looking for something slightly less energetic than martial arts then **Pilates** can really help, although it is surprising how good a work out you can get from this activity. Pilates involves mind-body conditioning through developing movement skills, focusing on core strength and endurance.

In conclusion all forms of physical activity can be beneficial to you for your skiing. The more effort you put in, prior to skiing, the more memorable your ski experience will be. Use some of the aforementioned ideas and get out and get fit 4 skiing!

## 4.2    Psychology & Skiing Performance

### Six steps for training the mind

So far this book has focused mostly on technical skiing, movements, balance etc. and physical preparation through cross training. However if you are to truly become great skiers then you must harness the power of the mind. What follows is a six step programme to help train the mind so that you can achieve truly great performance. These steps are as follows;

- Attitude
- Self-Talk
- Relaxation
- Imagery & Mental Rehearsal
- Pre-Performance Routines
- Peak Performance = Parallel Dreams

Aptitude together with the right attitude is the first step in achieving great performance. So in order to use psychology to aid you in your skiing performance you should start with developing the right attitude.

### Attitude

Attitude is important. But what you need to help you succeed is the right attitude. You have probably heard many terms associated with attitude such as; positive thinking, enthusiasm, positive perspective, optimism etc. All of these terms suggest that what you want is a positive attitude rather than a negative one. So do you have a choice over your attitude? I believe quite strongly that in most cases you do have a choice but you also need the right kind of input into your minds if this choice is to be made easier. In the words of Zig Ziglar, "You are what you are and where you are because of what has gone into your mind. You can change what you are; you can change where you are by changing what goes into your mind."

So if you want to improve your attitude then think about how much positive input you are getting versus negative input. You only have to watch the news regularly to top up your negative input! Try reading some good positive books or listening to some motivational recordings. In the same way as we watch what we eat, we need to think about our mental diet. Attitude is not permanent, whether good or bad. So to maintain a good, positive attitude you need to feed your mind with the right stuff.

Association is the key! You should also consider who you choose to spend time with. The people you hang out with tend to have an effect on you so if we want to be more positive choose people who are winners.

So a good mental diet combined with a careful choice of the people you spend time with, will greatly improve your chances of seeing things from a positive perspective. The famous comedian Billy Connolly sums this up beautifully with his quote, "There's no such thing as bad weather – only the wrong clothes, so get yourself a sexy raincoat and live a little."

Self-Talk

Some people say that they do not talk to themselves. Others say that talking to yourself is one of the first signs of madness! Well first of all you do all talk to yourself (we all do), but in many cases the voice in your head provides nothing but negative chat or worse still you end up arguing with yourself. Now that is madness!

What you need to do is get that little voice inside your head working for you not against you. This is where "Self-Talk" can help. Some practical examples of using self talk are; Positive Self Statements, Mood Words and Litanies.

**Positive self statements** are just that – a statement about your skiing that is personal to you, constructive and positive. An example would be, "I skied that last pitch really smoothly, now focus on rhythm and pole plant for this next pitch". These statements can relate to the past, present and future but its' important to keep in mind that you should **learn** from the past, **be** in the present and plan for the future. Keeping your thoughts in the present is usually the most effective and this is where **mood words** can be very useful. Words like smooth, attack, move, relax, quick, help to keep you focused on the task in hand and help you relate to the level of activation that you feel will help with achieving a great performance.

A **litany** is another form of self-talk and something that you can use away from the slopes. This is more to do with building self-esteem and can include personal statements as well as statements about your ability as a skier. For a litany to be effective you need to repeat it regularly.

Relaxation
---

Relaxation is both physical and mental and is the foundation for imagery and mental rehearsal. You can train yourself to relax and athletes use a range of techniques to help them become better at relaxing so that eventually they can do this quickly in the competition arena as part of a pre-competition strategy.

PMR – Progressive muscle relaxation is one of the most commonly used and easily learned techniques and was pioneered by Jacobson in 1939.

It involves deliberately tensing certain muscle groups and then releasing that tension and noticing how the muscles relax and the tension flows away. Through regular practice you quickly learn the feelings associated with tension and relaxation and you can then use this knowledge to recognise when you are becoming tense (and anxious) and therefore induce physical muscular relaxation. And physical relaxation is accompanied by mental calmness.

It is also a very inexpensive technique as all you require for practice is a recording (or your coach / instructor reading a script), that takes you through different muscle groups so that you can become familiar with the feelings of tension and relaxation throughout your entire body. To begin with this should be a fairly full programme, but as you practice this can be shortened until eventually you can quickly relax yourself both physically and mentally so that you are in a state of readiness for imagery and mental rehearsal.

One final point on PMR is that initial practice should be done in a quiet environment with no distractions. However eventually you will want to be able to use the technique as part of a pre-performance routine and therefore will need to be able to achieve this "state" in the skiing environment.

## Imagery & Mental Rehearsal

Imagery is a very powerful tool for sports people. It has been suggested through various studies that physical practice is better than mental practice. That mental practice is better than no practice at all. And that physical and mental practice when combined, produce the greatest results.

Some examples of imagery are as follows;
• Skill performance rehearsal
• Instant pre-play

- Instant re-play
- Performance review
- Confidence imagery
- "As if" imagery

**Skill performance rehearsal** involves the skier using imagery to practice the skill (movement pattern) that they wish to improve. This would normally be used away from the skiing environment (off snow).

**Instant pre-play** is used just before you execute a skill and is useful for regaining concentration and blocking out distractions. An example might be your first couple of turns down a steep couloir where success is of paramount importance!!

**Instant re-play** is, as it suggests, used just after you have performed a skill and is excellent for analysing your performance.

**Performance review** involves a re-run of all the key moments over a longer run and can involve how you felt in terms of aggression, relaxation, patience, calmness, focus etc. The intention here is to reinforce successful performances.

**Confidence imagery** involves recalling successful runs from the past where you were skiing at the peak of your performance. Again recalling feelings is vital here so that you can transfer them to your present situation and use them for inspiration.

**"As if" imagery** is more personal and subjective and involves you skiing as if you were someone who has attributes that you are trying to be associated with such as strength, agility, courage etc.

There are two ways in which you can "see" the image. a) From inside your body using your eyes (associated) or b) From outside as if watching a video (dissociated).

Using the associated method is excellent for tuning in all of your senses and feelings as if you are actually there doing the performance and helps to physically prepare the muscles for what they are about to do! This is ideal for **mental rehearsal** and should be imagined at normal speed rather than in slow motion. The great 1980's Swiss ski racer Pirmin Zurbriggen, was famously captured on TV going through his mental rehearsal, at the top of the race course, prior to one of his downhill world championships runs. They then showed this as an inset while simultaneously showing the actual run. The time taken for the mental rehearsal and the actual run were within one 100th of a second of each other. And it was the gold medal winning run!

The dissociated method can be used for fault correction in a similar way to how you use video playback. It is also useful if you want to dissociate yourself with any negative feelings. With some of the aforementioned types of imagery you might choose to move from dissociated to associated, depending on what you are trying to achieve. However the general advice is that associated imagery is the most powerful and should always be done at life speed, showing successful performances.

As with everything mentioned so far; attitude, self talk, relaxation and imagery you need to practice. Physical practice is great but combined with mental practice your chances of success greatly improve.

## Pre-Performance Routines

Competitive skiers commonly use pre- competition strategies. Whatever your involvement in the sport whether it be competitive skiing, instruction or recreational skiing there is great value in developing a strategy or "routine" that helps to ensure that you are ready to perform at your best.

Developing a pre-performance routine is a good way of encouraging consistency in your approach to skiing and will advocate the correct **mind set** and **focus of attention** that will most likely produce an effective performance.

Your routine should consider a range of aspects including; nutrition, rest & relaxation, preparation of equipment (skis, boots, sticks, clothing etc.) and warm up. The goal is to be physically and mentally prepared. And from a psychological point of view there is a lot of comfort to be taken from knowing that you have prepared well.

## Peak Performance = Parallel Dreams

The five previous steps have all been working towards helping you achieve "peak performances" by helping you to learn more about yourself and what makes you as individuals tick!

Your level of arousal (or stress) is the key to achieving those peak performance runs. If the level is too low you may simply not be activated enough to perform, while if the level is too high then fear or anxiousness may take over and ruin your skiing.

Achieving peak performances again and again takes practice and part of that practice should include the five previous steps. Technical competency in any sport is not enough. You need to be tactically aware, physically in good shape and of course mentally strong. Then you have every right to expect "Parallel Dreams"

Diagram 4a

# The Inverted U Theory

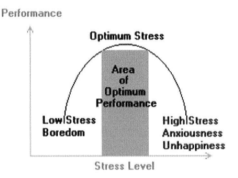

The Relationship Between Stress and Performance

In conclusion, psychology and skiing performance is a huge subject and the information that has been covered here is just scratching the surface of this important area and starting to give you some practical tools to help you to get your mind to work for you. If this is an area that interests you then I would recommend that you follow up on some of the references listed at the back of this book.

# Record of Notes, Thoughts & Ideas

*Siobhain Duggan tackling the steeps at la Flégère, Chamonix*
*Photo by Derek Tate*

# Segment 5 – And Finally

## 5.1    History of IASI

IASI was founded in 1989. Although a small organisation (currently with a membership of around 140) IASI has established itself on the international stage by becoming a member of ISIA, Interski, the Euro Group and IVSI (see the useful contacts near the end of this book for details on each of these organisations). Membership of IVSI was granted only recently in January 2007 and prompted a revamp of the whole training and grading structure with separate strands being developed for instructing and coaching complemented by a generic strand common to the other two.

The association has had a presence at several Interski Congresses and more recently has sent delegates to Norway in 1999 and Switzerland in 2003. The next congress will take place in St. Anton in Austria in 2011 and with the association going from strength to strength there is every prospect that IASI will have a bigger presence than ever perhaps even sending a demonstration team!

The association is run by a voluntary committee (now a Board of Directors) and has been chaired over the years by, Gerhard Mayrubher, Ronan Columb, Nadine Mangan, Alan Burns, Ian McGarry and most recently Deirdre O'Neill (who took office in September 2006).

As is the nature of modern sports associations IASI was incorporated as a limited company on the 19th of January 2001. The members of the association elect the Board of Directors, and these voluntary board members take care of the day to day activities of the association. At the start the role of the association was to assist the Ski Club of Ireland with the co-ordination of its artificial slope qualifications. However as the years passed there was a move (under the guidance of John Arnold) to run snow based courses and qualify members as full alpine ski instructors. Alongside this the qualification structure was developed (by Derek Tate) to match other international organisations. And last season the association ran courses in Hintertux, Austria and Chamonix, France with over six groups taking part in a range of modules. The association has now qualified 9 people to Level 3 ISIA and last March 2007 Siobhain Duggan became the first ever person to pass the Level 4 technical module (equivalent to the ISTD technical within the BASI system). Not only a great achievement for Siobhain, but also a milestone for IASI as it continues to grow.

With the enthusiasm of its members and commitment of its leadership the future is indeed bright for this small organisation.

*Team IASI at la Flégère, Chamonix*

*Photo by Derek Tate*

## 5.2    References

BASI. (2001). **Alpine Manual Version 2.0**. British Association of Snowsport Instructors.

Campbell, S., & Petrick, T. **Good Things to Know About Gliding on Snow**. Mountain Sports Press, Boulder, Colorado.

CSIA. (1995) **Skiing and Teaching Methods.** Canadian Ski Instructors' Alliance.

Egan, D. (1996). **All-Terrain Skiing**, Body Mechanics and Balance from Powder to Ice. A Joshua Tree Press Book.

Langmuir, S. (2006). **Knowledge is Power**, Biomechanics and your Ski Technique. BASI News article, spring 06

LeMaster, R. (1999). **The Skiers's Edge**. Human Kinetics.

Loudis, L. A., & Lobitz, W. C., & Singer, K. M. (1988). **Skiing Out of Your Mind**, The Psychology of Peak Performance. Springfield Books Limited.

Petersen, C. W. (2004). **Fit to Ski**. Published by Fit to Play, C.P.C. Physiotherapist Corp.

Shedden, J. (1986). **Skiing – Developing Your Skill.** The Crowood Press.

Shedden, J. (1982). **Skilful Skiing.** Published by EP Publishing Limited.

Witherell, W. (1972). **How the Racers Ski.** W. W. Norton & Company, Inc.

Ziglar, Z. (2000). **See You at the Top.** Revised. Pelican Publishing Company, Inc.

## 5.3    Useful Contacts

The following is a list of useful contacts for organisations and companies connected with the publication of this book.

**Anatom**
Importers for Backcountry Access (BCA) equipment
www.anatom.co.uk

**British Alpine Ski School (BASS) Chamonix**
Derek & Shona Tate's ski school
www.basschamonix.com

**British Alpine Ski & Snowboard School (BASS) Network**
Other BASS Ski Schools around the Alps
www.britishskischool.com

**Chill Factor[e]**
Indoor snow dome – an alpine village all year round
www.chillfactore.com

**International Ski Instructors Association (ISIA)**
International body for professional ski instructors
www.isiaski.org

**Interski**
Organisation for the Interski Congress (held every 4 years)
www.interski.org

**Irish Association of Snowsports Instructors (IASI)**
Professional Snowsports Qualifications
www.iasisnowsports.ie

**Internationaler Verband der Schneesportinstruktoren (IVSI)**
International body for amateur ski instructors
www.ivsi.de

**Outsider**
Ireland's Outdoor Magazine
www.outsider.ie

**Salomon Sports**
Snowsports Equipment & Clothing
www.salomonsports.com

**Ski Club of Ireland (SCI)**
Irelands' premier snowsports centre
www.skiclub.ie

**Snowsports Association of Ireland (SAI)**
National Governing Body
www.snowsports.ie

**Vew-Do Balance Boards**
Balance Training Equipment
www.vew-do.co.uk

**Wilderplaces**
Robbie Fenlon's company
www.wilderplaces.com

To order further copies of this book or to learn about
other Parallel Dreams publications check out;

**www.paralleldreams.co.uk**

The Parallel Dreams web site is the leading online
shop for skiing books and DVDs.

## 5.4 Index & Memorable Sayings

# Memorable Sayings

What follows are a few memorable and important sayings that have been used in writing this book. They are not necessarily attributed to the writers but are phrases that are commonly used by experts in the industry!

"Good fore / aft balance is achieved when you are supported by your bones through good skeletal alignment"

Segment 1.1 Balancing & Movements

"Stability versus agility is part of a compromise choice"

Segment 1.2 Biomechanical Principles

"Skiing can be thought of as a control and guidance activity, sliding down on a varying surface"

Segment 1.2 Biomechanical Principles

"Speed masks accuracy"

Segment 2.1 Core Skier Development

"Practice makes permanent", while "Correct practice makes perfect"

Segment 2.1 Core Skier Development

"Pivot not push" (PNP)

Segment 2.1 Core Skier Development<br>& 2.2 Skidding & Carving

"Tips together, tips apart"
> Segment 2.1 Core Skier Development

"Flow can be described as the icing on the cake"
> Segment 3.1 Performance on Piste

"Transceivers do not protect you from avalanches"
> Segment 3.3.2 Off Piste & Backcountry

"Association is the key"
> Segment 4.2 Psychology & Skiing Performance

*Dave Murrie enjoying the powder!*

*Photo by Nicola McDonnell*

# Record of Notes, Thoughts & Ideas

## Record of Notes, Thoughts & Ideas